SRA

Reading Mastery®

Transformations

Reading
Textbook A

Siegfried Engelmann

Susan Hanner

McGraw Hill

Acknowledgments

The authors are extremely grateful to Tina Wells for keeping the ship afloat on this project, and to Patricia McFadden, Margie Mayo, and Chris Gladfelter for their great attention to detail.

CREDITS

"Dream"
"Dream" from THE COLLECTED POEMS OF LANGSTON HUGHES by Langston Hughes, edited by Arnold Rampersad with David Roessel, Associate Editor, copyright © 1994 by the Estate of Langston Hughes. Used by permission of Alfred A. Knopf, an imprint of the Knopf Doubleday Publishing Group, a division of Penguin Random House LLC. All rights reserved. "Any third party use of this material, outside of this publication, is prohibited. Interested parties must apply directly to Penguin Random House LLC for permission."

"The Runner"
"The Runner" from A CARIBBEAN DOZEN. Copyright © 1994 Faustin Charles. Reproduced by permission of Candlewick Press, Somerville, MA, on behalf of Walker Books Ltd., London.

"Why Leopard Has Spots"
Paye, Won-Ldy, and Margaret H. Lippert. 1998. "Why Leopard Has Spots," In Why Leopard Has Spots: Dan Stories from Liberia, 3-5. Golden, CO: Fulcrum Publishing. Illustrations by McGraw-Hill Education. 2019.

"Boar Out There"
From EVERY LIVING THING by Cynthia Rylant. Text copyright © 1985 by Cynthia Rylant. Reprinted with the permission of Atheneum Books for Young Readers, an imprint of Simon & Schuster Children's Publishing Division. All rights reserved.

PHOTO CREDITS

014 Stocktrek Images, Inc./Alamy Stock Photo; **075** Stewart Myers/Shutterstock; **129** (tl)Mark Morgan/Alamy Stock Photo, (tr)Amazon-Images/Alamy Stock Photo, (b)WeatherVideoHD.TV; **141** Amazon-Images/Alamy Stock Photo; **145** (bl)WeatherVideoHD.TV, (bc)Amazon-Images/Alamy Stock Photo, (br)Mark Morgan/Alamy Stock Photo; **161** (l)Mark Morgan/Alamy Stock Photo, (c)Amazon-Images/Alamy Stock Photo, (r)WeatherVideoHD.TV; **163** (l)Ingram Publishing, (r)mevans/E+/Getty Images; **173** Amazon-Images/Alamy Stock Photo; **202** (l)Amazon-Images/Alamy Stock Photo, (c)Mark Morgan/Alamy Stock Photo, (r)WeatherVideoHD.TV; **215** Amazon-Images/Alamy Stock Photo; **253** (l)WeatherVideoHD.TV, (c)Amazon-Images/Alamy Stock Photo, (r)Mark Morgan/Alamy Stock Photo; **268** (t)Amazon-Images/Alamy Stock Photo; **286** Amazon-Images/Alamy Stock Photo; **317** Amazon-Images/Alamy Stock Photo.

mheducation.com/prek-12

Send all inquiries to:
McGraw-Hill Education
8787 Orion Place
Columbus, OH 43240

ISBN: 978-0-07-905418-0
MHID: 0-07-905418-8

Printed in the United States of America.

1 2 3 4 5 6 7 8 9 LWI 24 23 22 21 20

Table of Contents

Table of Contents

Table of Contents

A

1

1. female
2. select
3. migration
4. Florida
5. information

2

1. months
2. yearly
3. ponds
4. lonely
5. markings

3

1. Henry
2. chest
3. goose
4. geese
5. flapping

4

1. flock
2. male
3. migrate
4. shorter
5. hatch

Information About Geese

You're going to read a story about geese. Both geese and ducks are water birds, but geese are a lot bigger than ducks.

There are many different kinds of geese. Snow geese are white. The geese in the story you'll read are Canada geese. They are black, white, and brown.

The picture shows a person standing near some ducks, snow geese, and Canada geese. The picture also shows a flock of birds flying together.

Male geese and female geese have the same color and markings. But male geese are bigger than female geese.

Baby geese hatch from eggs that are a lot bigger than chicken eggs. The babies are born in spring. They are yellow, but as they grow older they change color. Geese are not full-grown by the time they are a year old.

When geese are three years old, they mate for the first time. Each female goose selects a mate, and the two geese stay together until one of them dies. As you will find out in the story, it may be a long time before one of them dies.

Old Henry

Lucas Novak

Chapter 1

A Goose Named Henry

The other geese called him Old Henry. His name tells you one thing about him. He was old. Most geese live about 30 years. That's a long time for a bird. But Old Henry was 35 years old.

You couldn't tell he was that old by looking at him. He was sort of black and brown with a white chest, just like the other Canada geese. If you saw Old Henry swimming on Big Trout Lake with the other geese on a warm summer day, you would not be able to tell that he was the oldest goose in the flock.

If you saw Old Henry three months later that year, you might get the idea that he was an old goose. ★ He was the only goose that was still on Big Trout Lake. All the other geese in the flock had gone south for the winter. They wanted Old Henry to go with them.

But he told them, "No, I'm getting too old to fly two thousand miles. I've done it too many times, and I'm just too tired."

The other geese told him, "But if you stay here, you may never make it through the winter. The lakes will freeze and you'll die."

Henry replied, "Maybe I won't die," but he didn't really believe that at all. So, he waved goodbye to the other geese as they took off from the lake, and he watched them form a great V that moved slowly south. He was alone and he felt sad.

GO TO PART A IN YOUR WORKBOOK

A

1	2	3
1. flocks	1. crooked	1. Crooked Lake
2. migration	2. yearly	2. Big Trout Lake
3. answers	3. sudden	3. Florida
4. flapping	4. breeze	4. Canada
5. fliers	5. migrate	
6. shorter	6. lonely	

B

More Information About Geese

Most wild geese are born in Canada and spend every summer in Canada. Geese live in flocks that may have more than 50 geese in them. In the fall, flocks fly south to their winter home. Then in the spring, they return to their summer home in Canada.

This yearly flying to the south and to the north is called a migration. When geese migrate in the fall, they fly south. In which direction do they migrate in the spring?

MAP 1

The geese that you're reading about migrate to a place in Florida. Map 2 shows the path of the migration from Big Trout Lake in Canada to Crooked Lake in Florida.

Geese migrate south in the fall because the lakes and rivers freeze in Canada. Farther south, lakes and rivers do not freeze.

Not all flocks migrate to the same place in the south. Some flocks migrate over three thousand miles to their winter home. Some migrate only a thousand miles.

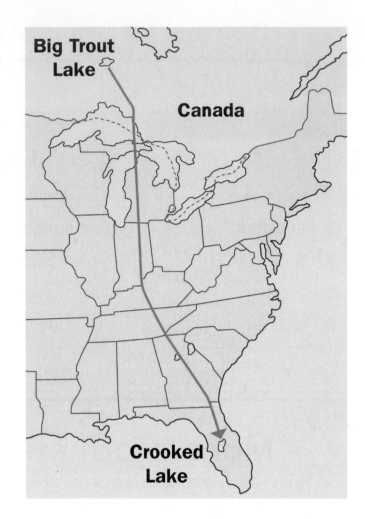

MAP 2

C Chapter 2

Henry Meets Tim

Henry stayed in Canada while the other geese in the flock went south for the winter. It was lonely being all alone on Big Trout Lake, but Henry had felt lonely for the last five years. That was when his wife died. Henry still missed her. She had been his mate since they were both three years old.

So Henry waited for winter. He spent time walking, swimming, and looking at the sky. Every now and then a flock of geese would fly by. Henry would listen to the leader as he honked directions to the other geese.

The days were getting shorter and colder. Henry knew that very soon Big Trout Lake would freeze. Nine days after the others had left, Old Henry saw another Canada goose walking along the shore.

Old Henry could tell that it was a very young goose. ⭐ It wasn't very big, and it didn't seem to know where it was going.

"Hey, there," Henry called. "What are you doing here? You're supposed to be on your way to Florida."

The young goose said, "Oh, I couldn't learn to fly because my leg was hurt."

Old Henry knew about that problem. When young geese learn to fly, they start out by running faster and faster. They hold their wings out to the sides as they run. Then they flap their wings and fly. But if they can't run fast, they can't fly. Later, geese learn to take off from the water, but that's not the first thing they learn about flying.

"Well," Henry said. "If you don't have anything better to do, swim out here and join me. I would be glad to have your company."

D REVIEW ITEMS

1. What's the name of geese that are black, brown, and white?

2. What's the name of geese that are all white?

3. What color are all geese when they are born?

4. You can tell male geese from female geese because ▨▨▨ .

   - male geese have brighter colors

   - male geese have longer feathers

   - male geese are larger

5. How old are geese when they mate for the first time?

6. After male and female geese mate, they stay together ▨▨▨ .

   - for the summer

   - for a full year

   - until one goose dies

7. Most geese live for about ▨▨▨ years.

8. What was the name of the lake where Henry's flock stayed during the summer?

9. In which season did the flock leave the lake?

10. In which direction did the flock fly?

11. How far was the flock going?

END OF LESSON 2

A

1
1. equator
2. extreme
3. flocks
4. breeze
5. above
6. fliers

2
1. glided
2. sudden
3. training
4. anymore
5. dived
6. answers

B

Directions on Maps

The geese in the story you're reading go from Canada to Florida in the fall. In which direction do they go?

In which direction do they go when they go from Florida to Canada?

Maps always show four directions—north, south, east, and west.

North is always at the top of the map.

South is always at the bottom of the map.

East is always on this side of the map. ⟶

West is always on this side of the map. ⟵

Map A shows the directions on all maps.

Touch the circle in the middle of the map and move your finger to the top of the map. In which direction did you go?

Touch the circle and move to the bottom of the map. In which direction did you go?

Touch the circle and move to the number **2.** In which direction did you go?

Touch the circle and move to the **4.** In which direction did you go?

MAP A

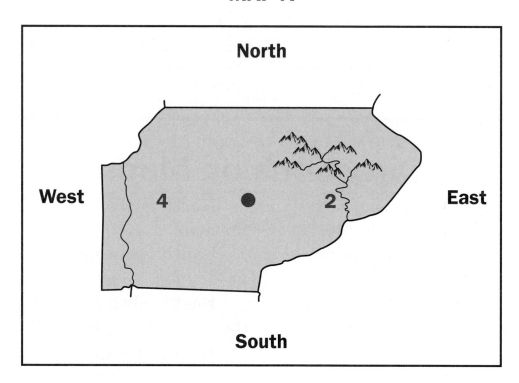

North

West

4

2

East

South

Map B shows Canada, the United States, and some other countries.

Is the red dot in the United States, or in Canada? In which country is the blue dot?

Touch the red dot and go to the **4** on the map. In which direction did you go?

Touch the red dot and go to the **3**. In which direction did you go?

The red dot is in the United States. What's the name of the **state** the red dot is in?

MAP B

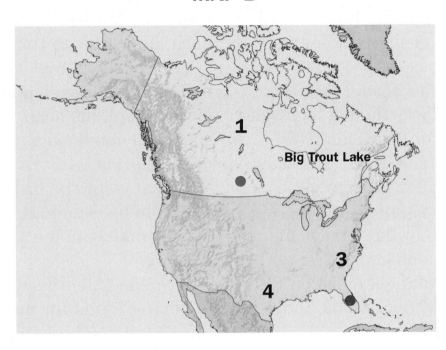

Tim's Questions

Old Henry and a young goose were the only ones left on a pond in Canada. The young goose swam up to Old Henry and said, "My name is Tim. What's your name?"

Henry answered Tim's question, and then Tim said, "I have a lot of questions about geese. I was never able to ask my mom these questions because she was so busy getting my brothers and sisters ready for the flight down south."

Henry said, "So you have never made the trip to the south."

"That's right," Tim said. "I was born last June. So I'm less than half a year old."

"Well, ask me the questions," Old Henry said, "and I'll tell you the answers."

Tim said, "Well, Mom always told us that geese are the best high fliers there are. I don't know what she meant by that."

Old Henry laughed and said, "On the other side of the world are some mountains that are over five miles high. There's only one kind of bird that can fly over those mountains, and that's a goose."

Tim shook his head. "Wow," he said. "Do the flocks fly that high when they go south for the winter?" ⭐

"No, no," Henry said. "You only go that high if you have to get over something. We fly pretty high, sometimes two or three miles high, but that's about as high as we go."

"I can see that geese fly pretty fast," Tim said, "but do you know how fast they go?"

"Of course I know," Old Henry said. "Geese can fly one mile a minute. That's sixty miles per hour, and geese can fly at that speed all day long."

The geese stopped talking as a sudden breeze blew across the lake. It was very cold. Henry shook his head and said, "There will be some ice on Big Trout Lake tomorrow morning."

Tim said, "I wish I could fly south. My leg feels better now, but I don't know how to fly."

Henry said, "Well, if your leg is better, I could teach you how to fly." Henry shook his head. "And I suppose I could even tell you how to get to Florida."

"That would be great," Tim said. "It would be even better if you would come with me and show me the way."

"No, no," Henry said. "I have flown to Florida for the last time. But I'll tell you how to get there."

"Thank you," Tim said. "I would really love to go there."

D REVIEW ITEMS

1. What's the name of geese that are all white?

2. What's the name of geese that are black, brown, and white?

3. What color are all geese when they are born?

4. How old are geese when they mate for the first time?

5. After male and female geese mate, how long do they stay together?

6. Most geese live for about ▨▨▨ years.

7. Geese live in large groups called ▨▨▨ .

8. Where are most wild geese born?

---

9. In which direction do geese fly in the fall?

10. What is this trip called?

- migration

- mating

- vacation

---

11. How had Henry felt ever since his wife had died?

---

12. When geese learn to fly, do they start in the water or on the land?

13. They run with their ▨▨▨ out to the side.

END OF LESSON 3

4

A

1
1. route
2. receive
3. unfrozen
4. above
5. equator
6. anymore

2
1. barns
2. glided
3. circles
4. proudly
5. dived

3
1. extreme
2. extremely
3. training
4. space
5. spaceship

B

Information About the Earth

Some places on the earth are colder and some places are hotter. Here are some facts you need to know about the earth.

- The earth is shaped like a ball. It doesn't look like it's that shape because the earth is very large. When you look at the earth from a spaceship, it looks like a ball.

- The earth slowly turns around and around.

PICTURE 1

- The equator is a pretend line that goes around the fattest part of the earth.
- The equator is the hottest part of the earth.
- The pretend lines on the top and bottom of the earth are the poles. The top pole is called the North Pole. The bottom pole is called the South Pole.
- The farther you go from the equator, the colder you get.
- The poles are the parts of the earth that are farthest from the equator. That's why the poles are the coldest parts of the earth.

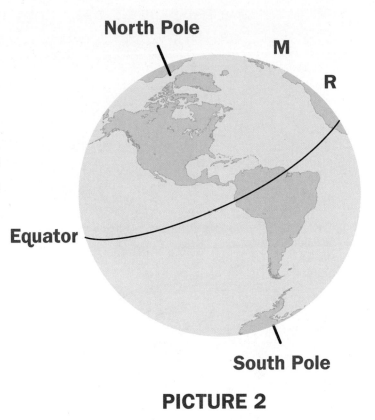

PICTURE 2

Tim Has a Flying Lesson

Ice had formed all around the shore of the lake, and the morning was very cold and still. Tim said, "Wow, it's really cold this morning."

"Yes," Old Henry said, "and if you're going to get on your way to Florida before it gets even colder, we'd better start on your training today."

So Henry explained what Tim had to do. He had to run with his wings held straight out to the sides. Then Henry would honk, which would tell Tim to start flapping his wings. "I'll bet you can do it the first time you try," Henry said.

Henry and Tim went to a hill near the lake. Henry said, "Just run down this hill as fast as you can, and remember to keep those wings out to the side."

Then Henry took off and circled above Tim. "Go," Henry said, and Tim went—running as fast as he could.

Henry honked and Tim started flapping his wings. "That's it," Henry honked. "Keep flapping."

Tim took off, but as soon as he did, he became frightened and stopped flapping. Plop. He fell back down to the ground and tumbled over and over.

Henry landed next to him, laughed, then said, "At least you got into the air. Now all you have to do is learn how to stay up there. To do that you have to keep flapping after you take off." ★

Tim said, "That's what I wanted to do, but I got scared."

Henry said, "Well, just remember: Geese are made for flying. It's nothing to be scared about. I'll fly in front of you. Just keep looking at me and do what I do."

So they tried again. This time, Henry made sure that he was right in front of Tim when he took off. Henry honked and honked. He shouted, "Keep flapping and look at me."

The two geese flew all the way across the lake and over the hill on the other side. Henry turned around to look at Tim. He didn't look scared anymore, because he had a big smile on his face. He honked, "This is great. I love it."

"Well, just keep doing what I do," Henry said.

Henry led Tim up higher and higher, more than a mile high. Then Henry held his wings out to the sides and glided. As Tim followed him, the birds turned and swooped and dived and climbed. At last Henry said, "Now we're going to land. We'll go in the water. Remember to do what I do."

Henry came down and made a perfect landing in the water. Tim also made a landing, but it was not perfect. He was going too fast, and he landed with a great splash. Both geese laughed. Tim shouted proudly, "I can fly."

"You sure can," Henry said.

Number your paper from 1 through 11.

D REVIEW ITEMS

1. You can tell male geese from female geese because   .

   - male geese are larger

   - male geese have brighter colors

   - male geese have longer feathers

2. What was the name of the lake where Henry's flock stayed during the summer?

3. In which season did the flock leave the lake?

4. In which direction did the flock fly?

5. How far was the flock going?

6. Geese live in large groups called   .

7. Where are most wild geese born?

Look at the map.

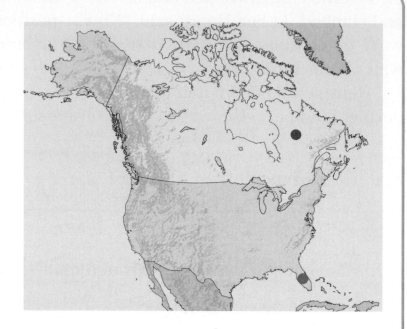

8. What country is the red dot in?

9. What country is the blue dot in?

10. What **state** is the blue dot in?

11. If you started at the red dot and went to the blue dot, in which direction would you go?

END OF LESSON 4

A

1
1. dangers
2. receives
3. barns
4. circles
5. lakes

2
1. foolish
2. below
3. daytime
4. unfrozen
5. dangerous
6. restless

3
1. trout
2. sprang
3. route
4. neck
5. confused

B

Information About the Equator

You've learned about the poles and the equator. Let's see how much you remember.

- How many poles are there?
- What are they called?

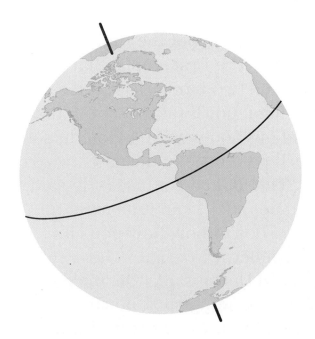

- What do we call the line that goes around the fattest part of the earth?
- Where is the hottest part of the earth?
- Which parts of the earth are the coldest?

The heat that the earth receives comes from the sun. The equator is the hottest part of the earth because it receives more heat from the sun than any other place on the earth. The poles are the coldest places on the earth because they receive less heat from the sun than any other place on the earth.

Tim Practices Flying

The two geese spent most of the next three days flying. Tim needed the practice, and Old Henry felt warmer when he was flying rather than swimming on that lake. There wasn't much room to swim anymore because most of the lake was frozen. Only some small circles near the middle were unfrozen. So Tim practiced and Old Henry gave him directions. By the third day, Tim could land on land and in the water. He still had trouble taking off from the water, but he could do it.

As the sun was setting on the third day, Old Henry said, "Well, my boy, the lake will be completely frozen tomorrow, so tomorrow is the time for you to go south."

Old Henry started to tell Tim how to get to Florida. The route was not simple. There were landing places about every 300 miles. Tim would have to land at each place and spend one or two nights. Then he would take off and go to the next landing place. Old Henry started to tell Tim about each landing place. But Tim had trouble understanding the directions.

Old Henry started out by saying, "You take off from this lake and fly south and east. By about the middle of the afternoon, you'll come to a field that is next to a pond. The field has two barns. One is red and ..."

Tim said, "I don't know which way south is."

"Of course you do," Henry said. "All geese know north from south."

"But I ..." Tim said.

Henry said, "Do this for me. ★ Take off, go high, and go in the direction that feels really good. Fly in that direction for a little while and then come back here."

Tim went up and circled around and then he started flying directly south. Soon he came back and landed next to Henry.

Henry said, "You were flying south. All geese like that direction in the fall. In the spring, they like the opposite direction, north."

Then Henry said, "Let's talk some more about the flight to Florida. The first stop is that field with the two barns. The next morning, you'll take off from that field but you won't fly exactly south. You'll go a little to the east."

Tim looked confused. He said, "I'm not sure I can remember all this. I don't know how you can remember it."

Old Henry said, "Oh, once you go to a landing spot, you'll remember it for the rest of your life.

You'll know exactly how to get there and exactly what it looks like."

Then Old Henry tried again to tell Tim about the landing places. But by the time Henry had explained how to reach the third one, he could see that Tim was just about ready to start crying. "I'm sorry," Tim said, "but I just can't keep all this straight.

How many landing places are there between here and Florida?"

Old Henry said, "Five," and Tim got a big tear in his eye.

"I can't do it," Tim said. "I'll never remember how to get there."

Old Henry said, "Well, we'll figure out some way to get you there."

Number your paper from 1 through 16.

D REVIEW ITEMS

Look at the map below.

1. What country is the green dot in?
2. What country is the purple dot in?
3. What state is the purple dot in?
4. If you started at the purple dot and went to the green dot, in which direction would you go?

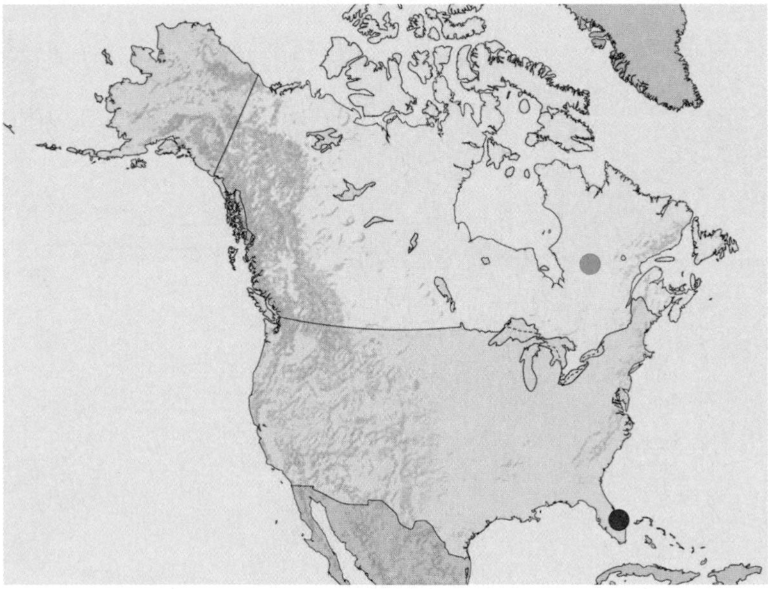

5. The earth is shaped like a ______ .
6. The hottest part of the earth is called the ______ .
   - pole
   - desert
   - equator
7. What's the name of the line that goes around the fattest part of the earth?
8. What's the name of the spot that's at the top of the earth?
9. What's the name of the spot that's at the bottom of the earth?

10. The ▓▓▓s are the coldest places on the earth and the ▓▓▓ is the hottest place on the earth.

11. How many poles are there?

12. The farther you go from the equator, the ▓▓▓ you get.

- hotter
- fatter
- colder

Look at the map below.

13. What's the name of the place shown by the letter **C?**

14. Which letter shows the coldest place?

15. Which letter shows the hottest place?

16. Which letter is farthest from the equator?

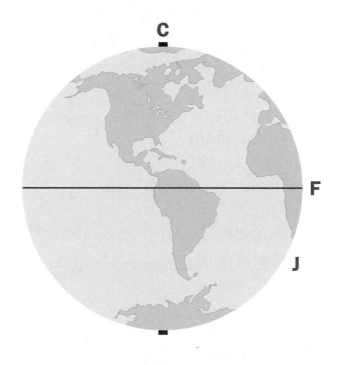

A

1
1. Michigan
2. Kentucky
3. crooked
4. cause
5. triangle
6. effect

2
1. foolish
2. dangers
3. rivers
4. sharper
5. lakes
6. fighter

3
1. trout
2. daytime
3. nighttime
4. below
5. sprang
6. fake

B

The Sun Lights the Earth

The sun shines all the time. But you can't see the sun all the time. Only half of the earth is in sunlight. You can see the sun if you're on the side of the earth that is closer to the sun. It is daytime on the side of the earth where you can see the sun. It is nighttime on the side of the earth where you can't see the sun.

It takes the earth 24 hours to turn around one time. Part of that 24 hours is nighttime, and the other part of that 24 hours is daytime.

PICTURE A

PICTURE B

The Geese Leave Big Trout Lake

Tim and Old Henry spent the night in a small woods near the lake. In the morning, the lake was completely frozen and the air was even colder than it had been.

Tim said, "I'm supposed to leave today. But I still don't know about all the landing spots. How long do you think it's going to take for me to learn about them?"

Henry said, "Oh, I thought of a different plan. I'll fly along with you part of the way. After we reach the third landing place, I'll head back here."

Tim smiled. "Thank you," he said. "I like this plan a lot better."

"Well, let's get going then," Henry said. "And remember to follow all the directions I honk out."

"I will," Tim said. And the two geese took off, circled above Big Trout Lake one time, and then headed south.

Old Henry led the way and Tim followed. But Tim got tired after the geese had flown about sixty miles. As they flew over a large lake, Tim said, "Let's land down there for a while. I see a few geese near the shore."

Old Henry laughed and said, "Never land where you see only a few geese. You'll find out they are not real geese at all. They are fake geese that hunters use to make other geese think it is safe to land there. But most of the geese that try to land there will get shot."

"Well, where can we land?"

"Two kinds of places are safe," Henry said. "One kind of safe place has hundreds of geese on the water. Another kind of safe place has no geese on the water." Then Henry said, "Pick a safe place for us to land."

Tim said, "That's easy. There are lots of lakes down there, and I don't see ducks or geese on most of them."

"Well, lead the way to a safe place then." And that's what Tim did. The two geese rested there for a while. ★ They ate some water plants and took a nap in a field. Then they took off and flew south again. A few hours later the two geese flew over the landing place where they would spend the night. Old Henry didn't say anything about where they were. He wanted to see if Tim would recognize the place. He didn't. Henry asked him, "Do you see anything interesting down below us?"

Tim looked at the trees, the pond, and the two barns in the field. Then he said, "No, what's interesting down there?"

At that moment, Old Henry knew that he would have to do something more than just tell Tim about how to get to Florida on his own.

The geese landed near the barns. They were empty except for some mice that lived in them. Something didn't smell right to Henry, however. Something told him to get out of this place. Just then, a red fox sprang from the grass and charged toward Tim. Before Tim could take off, the fox had grabbed his tail feathers. "Help," Tim yelled.

Old Henry put his head down and charged at the fox. He bit the fox on the neck and ears. The fox tried to attack Old Henry, but Old Henry kept biting the fox until it ran away.

Henry looked at where the fox had grabbed Tim to make sure that Tim was not hurt. Tim was all right.

Then Old Henry said, "That was a foolish fox. I guess she doesn't know that a full-grown goose is a much better fighter than a fox."

What Henry didn't tell Tim was that an old goose that tries to fight a fox might hurt itself. Old Henry had a very sore wing. He was glad that he wouldn't have to fly until the morning.

Tim and Henry walked all around to make sure that no other dangers were near the barn. Henry told Tim, "I think it will be safe here if we spend the night in one of these barns." And that's what the geese did.

Number your paper from 1 through 20.

STORY ITEMS

1. Where did Henry and Tim spend their last night at Big Trout Lake?

   • on the water   • in a barn   • in the woods

2. In the morning, Henry told Tim that he would ▭ .

   • tell Tim more about the trip   • fly part of the way with him

3. Henry told Tim, "Don't land where you see ▭ ."

   • many geese   • a few geese   • no geese

4. Write the letters of the **2** kinds of places that are safe for geese.

   a. places with many geese

   b. places with no geese or ducks

   c. places with a few geese

   d. places with a few ducks

5. When the two geese flew over the landing place, did Tim recognize it?

6. After they landed, which goose was attacked?

7. What attacked that goose?

8. What did Henry do?

9. Which is a better fighter, a full-grown goose or a fox?

10. After the fight, Henry had a sore ▨ .

E REVIEW ITEMS

11. How old are geese when they mate for the first time?

12. After male and female geese mate, how long do they stay together?

13. Most geese live for about ▨ years.

Choose from these words to answer each item:

- moon
- Florida
- sun
- Canada
- equator
- geese
- poles
- migration

14. The heat that the earth receives comes from the ▨ .

15. The part of the earth that receives more heat than any other part is the ▨ .

16. The parts of the earth that receive less heat than any other part are called the ▨ .

17. Which letter shows the part of the earth that receives more heat from the sun than any other letter?

18. Which letter shows a part of the earth that receives less heat from the sun than any other letter?

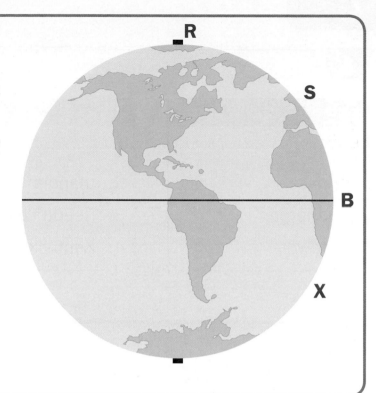

19. How many landing places are there on Henry's migration trip to Florida?

20. Was Tim able to understand what Henry explained about the landing places?

END OF LESSON 6

1	**2**	**3**
1. older	1. key	1. crooked
2. river	2. triangle	2. effect
3. sharper	3. Reedy Lake	3. Michigan
4. fewer	4. Kentucky	4. cause

B

Michigan and Kentucky

The map shows the migration path the geese are following. The map also shows the first three landing places.

Touch Big Trout Lake and go to dot 1. That's the first landing place.

What country is that landing place in?

Touch dot 1 and go to dot 2. That's the second landing place.

That landing place is in the United States. It is in a state named Michigan.

Touch the landing place in Michigan and go to dot 3. That's the next landing place.

That landing place is not in the state of Michigan. It is in the state of Kentucky.

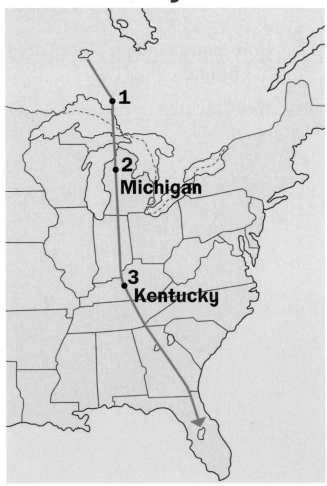

Old Henry Tests Tim

Old Henry's wing was very sore the next morning, but he didn't tell Tim about it. Before the geese took off, Old Henry tried to explain the next landing place to Tim. It was a field that had a stream running through it. The field was shaped like a triangle, and the field had a large grove of trees on the east side of the triangle. Old Henry even scratched a map in the dirt that showed the landing place, the stream, and the trees. "Remember, that's the place we're looking for this afternoon," Henry said, "but I won't tell you when we get there. You'll have to tell me when we're there."

Henry didn't know how well Tim would do, but Henry had to find out. He knew that Tim didn't learn if Henry just described the place. But Henry hoped that Tim would do better if he saw a map.

So the geese took off and flew south. About an hour before they came to the landing place, Old Henry tested Tim by saying, "Look down there and tell me if you see anything that is interesting."

Tim looked down and then looked at Old Henry. Tim said, "I think that's where we are supposed to land for tonight. Am I right?"

"No," Old Henry said. "That is not the place."

Tim said, "I'm sorry. I guess I can't find these places because I am not very smart."

"You're doing fine," Henry said, but Tim was not doing fine. An hour later the geese flew over the stream and the field shaped like a triangle. After they had flown past it, Old Henry said, "Our landing place is back there. Follow me." He knew that Tim would not be able to make the rest of the trip unless Henry flew with him.

After the geese had landed, Henry said, "What if we wanted to go back to our first landing place? ★ Could you find the way back?"

"Oh, sure," Tim said. "That's easy. You just fly back that way until you come to some blue hills, then you turn a little and go more north until you come to the place where the two rivers cross …" Tim went on to tell all the important facts about how to get there.

Old Henry spent a lot of time thinking that night, and he thought a lot more the next day. The geese did not fly on that day or on the day after that. On the first day, they rested and talked. It was warmer here than it had been farther north. The geese were not in Canada anymore. They were in Michigan where the trees were yellow and orange and the sun was warm.

Old Henry knew that Tim could not remember a place unless he went to that place. So somebody would have to lead him all the way to Florida. Henry's problem was that his wing felt worse than ever. Henry didn't know how much more of the trip he would be able to make.

Tim and Henry rested a second day. That day was the first time they saw another flock of geese, which formed a great V in the sky. Both Henry and Tim had eyes far sharper than human eyes, so they were able to see all the geese in that flock. Henry said, "There must be more than 60 geese in that flock."

"Are they going to the same place we're going?" Tim asked.

"No," Henry said. "They are heading a little bit to the west, so they are probably going all the way to Mexico."

Tim asked, "Have you ever been to Mexico?"

Henry said, "No. The only place I've ever gone in the winter is to Crooked Lake in Florida. And that's what you'll do. Every year, you'll fly to Crooked Lake, and in the spring you'll fly back to Canada."

Number your paper from 1 through 13.

D REVIEW ITEMS

1. The sun shines _____ .
   - all of the time
   - some of the time
2. Can you see the sun all day long and all night long?
3. If you cannot see the sun, it is _____ on your side of the earth.
4. What is it on the other side of the earth?
5. The earth turns around one time every _____ hours.

6. Write the letters of the **2** kinds of places that are safe for geese.

    a. places with many geese

    b. places with a few geese

    c. places with no geese or ducks

    d. places with a few ducks

Look at the picture.

7. Which side of the earth is closer to the sun, **A** or **B**?

8. Which side of the earth is in nighttime?

9. Which side of the earth is in daytime?

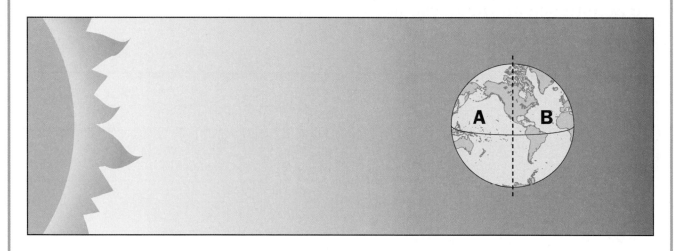

10. Which letter shows the place that has the warmest winters?

11. Which letter shows the place that is closest to the equator?

12. Which letter shows the place that is closest to a pole?

13. Is the **North Pole** or the **South Pole** closer to that letter?

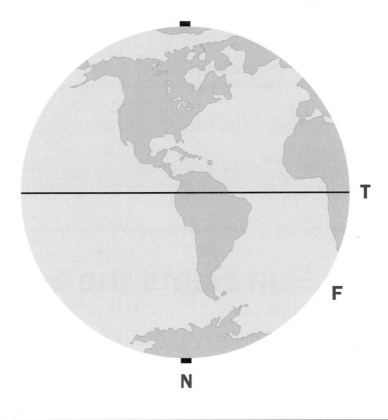

A

1	2
1. <u>few</u>er	1. Reedy Lake
2. <u>sea</u>son	2. Clarks Hill Lake
3. <u>hurt</u>ing	3. Jackson Lake
4. <u>cloud</u>y	4. shown
5. <u>old</u>er	
6. <u>eigh</u>ty	

B

The Sun Heats the Earth

You can figure out which parts of the earth are hot and which are cold if you look at how the light from the sun gets to the earth.

The picture shows lines of heat that are going from the sun to the earth. Those lines are the same distance apart.

Here's a rule about the lines of heat: **Places on the earth that have more lines of heat are hotter than places that have fewer lines of heat.**

Places A, B, and C on the earth are the same size, but one of them is a very hot place and one is a very

cold place. The hot place receives more lines of heat from the sun. So if you want to find out which place has more heat, you count the number of lines from the sun that hit that place.

Count the lines that hit place C. Count the lines of heat at place B. Count the lines of heat at place A. Remember, the sun heats the earth, and the equator receives more heat than any other part of the earth.

C **Chapter 8**

A New Plan

The next day's flight was very hard on Old Henry. His wing was sore, and the next landing place was a little more than 300 miles south of the landing place in Michigan. It would have made sense for the geese to travel only 200 miles and then spend the night at a new landing place. But geese don't always make sense. They always go to the same landing places. If those places are a little more than 300 miles apart, the geese fly a little more than 300 miles.

Tim and Old Henry reached the landing place by late afternoon. This landing place was between two lakes in Kentucky. One was large and one was small. Something about the large lake didn't seem right to Old Henry. There were some geese on the large lake, but they were too close to the shore.

Henry's wing was so sore that he really wanted to land and rest. So he told himself, "There's no problem down there," and he started to lead the way down to where the other geese were swimming.

Tim flew up next to Old Henry and said, "I don't think we should land there."

"Why not?"

"You told me never to land in a place that had only a few geese on the water." Just then the geese heard a sound that was something like another goose calling, but Old Henry knew that it was not the sound of a real goose.

He said, "You're right, Tim. There are hunters down there. Let's get out of here."

The geese made a great turn and started to climb higher and higher into the sky. Just then, there were loud banging sounds. Hunters were shooting at Tim and Old Henry, but they were too far away. "You may have saved our lives," Henry said to Tim. "You're a very smart young goose."

The two geese found another landing place about five miles away. 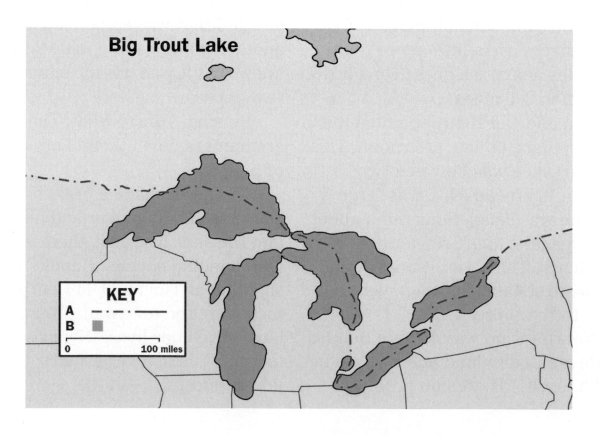 It was a field that had a small pond in the middle of it. The geese landed, took a nap, and then ate some seeds. Old Henry wanted to go the rest of the way to Florida, but he knew that he could not travel as fast as flocks usually go. If Henry was going to make it, he would have to fly one day and rest the next. He couldn't fly two days in a row.

When the sun was growing red in the west sky, the two geese were sitting near the pond. Tim said, "So where do we go tomorrow?"

Henry told him the plan. "We're going to rest tomorrow. Then we'll fly the next day."

Tim said, "But I'm not tired. I'll be ready to fly tomorrow."

"I won't be ready," Henry said.

Tim looked at Henry for a long time. Then he said, "Well, you're in charge. Anything you want to do is fine with me."

So the birds rested the next day. Late that afternoon, a large flock of more than eighty geese landed near the pond. The leader of the flock and three of the older geese came over and talked to Henry and Tim.

The leader asked, "Where's the rest of your flock?"

Old Henry explained where the rest of the flock was and why Tim hadn't gone with them.

The leader of the other flock said, "We're from one of the big lakes between Canada and the United States."

Big Trout Lake

KEY

A – ·– ·– ·–

B ■

0   100 miles

Tim said, "I know those big lakes. We flew over one of them, didn't we, Henry?"

"Yes, we did," Henry said. Then he asked the leader, "Are you on your way to Florida?"

"We are," the leader said. "We go to Reedy Lake."

"That's wonderful," Old Henry said. "Tim is trying to go to Crooked Lake."

"Oh," the leader said. "That's only a few miles from Reedy Lake."

Old Henry said, "How would it be if Tim went with your flock? You could drop him off at Crooked Lake."

"We could do that," the leader said.

Number your paper from 1 through 28.

D INFORMATION ITEMS

1. How many heat lines are hitting place A on the map?

2. How many heat lines are hitting place B?

3. How many heat lines are hitting place C?

4. Write the letter of the place that is the hottest.

5. Write the letter of the place that's the coldest.

6. Write the letter of the place that has the warmest winters.

7. Write the letter of the place that's the farthest from the equator.

8. You know that place A is hotter than place C because place A ▮▮▮▮ .

   • is closer to the poles
   • is in sunlight
   • has more lines of heat

STORY ITEMS

9. About how far was it from the landing place in Michigan to the one in Kentucky?

10. How did Henry feel by the end of that trip?

11. Which goose wanted to land at the regular landing place in Kentucky?

12. What kept them from landing there?

    - The lake was frozen.
    - Hunters were at that landing place.
    - Too many geese were at that landing place.

13. Henry and Tim landed at a place that was about ▬▬ miles away.

14. Did Henry plan to stay at this landing place **one day** or **two days**?

15. Another ▬▬ landed at the landing place the next day.

16. How many geese were in that flock?

17. Where was that flock going?

18. That flock spent summers on one of the big lakes between ▬▬ and the United States.

19. Henry asked if ▬▬ could fly with that flock.

20. Did the leader of that flock think this plan was okay?

F **REVIEW ITEMS**

21. In which direction do geese fly in the fall?

22. What is this trip called?

23. At which letter would the winters be very, very cold?

24. At which letter would the winters by very, very hot?

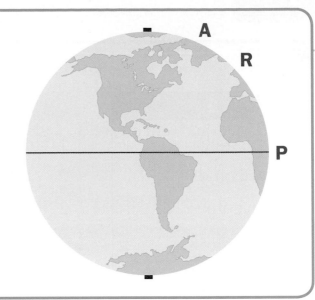

25. Write the letter of the earth that shows the person in daytime.

26. Write the letter of the earth that shows the person 6 hours later.

27. Write the letter that shows the person another 6 hours later.

28. Write the letter that shows the person another 6 hours later.

END OF LESSON 8

A

1
1. constant
2. welcome
3. seventy
4. daylight
5. wintertime

2
1. tilted
2. cloudy
3. friends
4. hardest
5. reaches
6. honking

3
1. South Carolina
2. Georgia
3. Newnans Lake
4. Jackson Lake
5. Clarks Hill Lake

B

Information About the Sun and the Earth

Here's a rule about the earth and the sun. The earth is moving around the sun all the time. The earth makes a complete circle around the sun one time every year. A year is 365 days, so it takes the earth 365 days to make a complete circle around the sun.

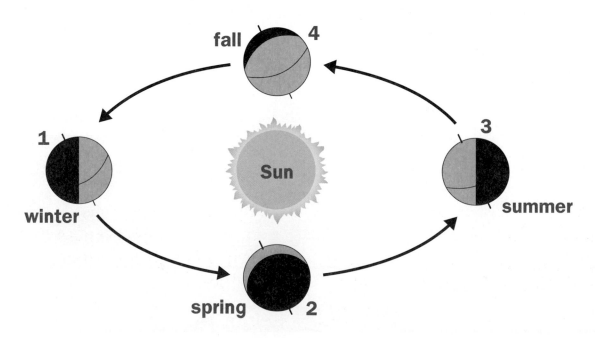

The picture shows the earth at four different times of the year as it circles the sun.

Touch the picture of the earth during winter.

Follow the arrow around the sun and name the season that is shown by each earth. Start with the earth at wintertime.

Remember, the earth is in different places at different seasons of the year.

C Chapter 9

Flying with the Flock

After the geese from the large flock finished talking with Old Henry, they went over to their flock. As soon as they had left, Tim said, "When is that other flock going to fly?"

"Tomorrow," Henry said.

"We planned to fly tomorrow, didn't we?"

"Yes," Henry said.

"Well, why did you say I would fly with them? I thought I was flying with you."

Old Henry said, "Tim, I'm not sure I can make it all the way to Florida. If you go with them, they'll drop you off at Crooked Lake."

"But what will you do?" Tim asked. "Aren't you going to fly with them, too?"

"Well . . ." Old Henry said. He wanted to tell Tim that he didn't plan to go any farther south, but Tim looked very sad. So Old Henry said, "Well, I'll go with them as far as I can. I'll fly with them tomorrow and then I'll see how I feel at the end of the day."

"Well, I'm going where you go," Tim said. "If you fly with them after tomorrow, I'll fly with them. But if you don't fly with them after tomorrow, I won't fly with them."

"We'll see how it goes tomorrow," Henry said.

So the next morning, more than eighty geese took off from that pond in Kentucky and formed a great V in the sky. The leader was near the front of the V, but he was not at the very point of the V. He was back a few places so he could see the front of the V and honk out orders to the other geese. Old Henry and Tim were far behind the leader. Tim was right behind a young goose. Old Henry was in front of one of the older geese.

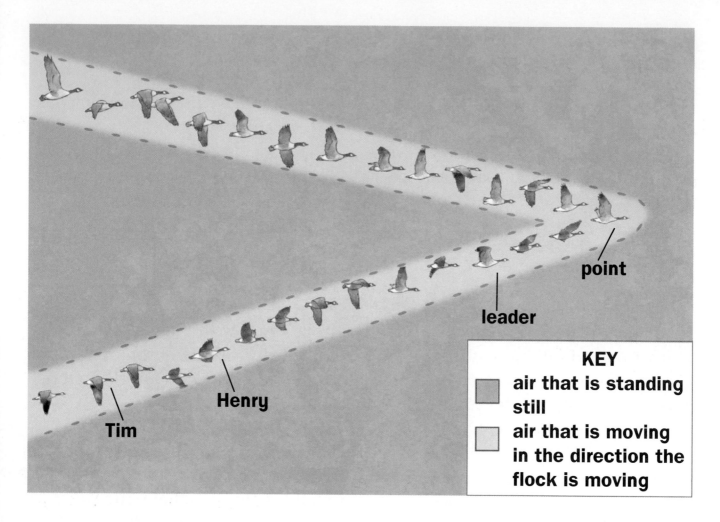

After the flock stopped climbing, it was nearly two miles high. ✦ Tim called out to Henry, "I notice that it is a lot easier to fly than it was when you and I were alone."

"Right," Henry said. "It's easier flying in a large flock."

"Why?"

✿ Old Henry explained. "We are behind a lot of other geese. Those geese fly through the air and leave a trail of wind that moves in the same direction the geese are moving. We're flying through that air, so we don't have to work as hard as the geese up front."

Tim said, "That's good for us, but I sure wouldn't want to be one of those geese up front."

Henry said, "All the geese that are up front take turns at being the first goose in the V. They fly at the point for an hour or more and then change places with another goose."

Then Henry noticed that his wing wasn't as sore ✿ as it had been. He hadn't been thinking about that wing because it hadn't been hurting. Henry realized that it hadn't been hurting because it didn't have to work as hard as it did when he and Tim flew alone.

Henry said to himself, "If it doesn't get any harder than this, maybe . . ." He still wasn't sure how he would feel the next morning when the rest of the flock was ready to fly again.

Later that afternoon, when the sky was starting to get very cloudy, the great V of geese went lower and lower through the clouds and came out of them above a beautiful green lake. Tim asked Henry, "What's that lake?"

Henry said, "I don't know. This is not on the route I've taken. We always land at Clarks Hill Lake. It's much bigger than this lake and it's farther east."

Then Henry asked the old goose behind him, "What's the name of that lake?"

"Jackson Lake."

About ten minutes later the flock landed on Jackson Lake.

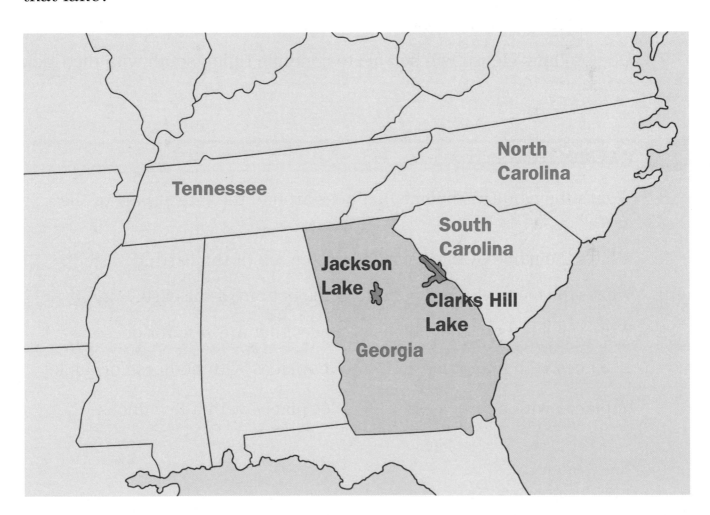

D STORY ITEMS

1. Henry noticed that his wing felt ▨▨▨ because it didn't have to work very ▨▨▨ .

2. What's the name of the lake where the flock landed?

3. In what state is that lake?

4. Had Henry landed there before?

5. At what lake did Henry's flock usually land?

6. Which lake is farther east?

7. Do you think Henry will be able to continue flying south with the flock in chapter 10?

E REVIEW ITEMS

8. What's the name of the line that goes around the fattest part of the earth?

9. What's the name of the spot that's at the top of the earth?

10. What's the name of the spot that's at the bottom of the earth?

11. Write the letters of the 2 kinds of places that are safe for geese.

    a. places with many geese   c. places with no geese or ducks

    b. places with a few geese   d. places with a few ducks

12. How many heat lines are hitting place A on the map?

13. How many heat lines are hitting place B?

14. How many heat lines are hitting place C?

15. Write the letter of the place that's the hottest.

16. Write the letter of the place that's the coldest.

17. Write the letter of the place that has the warmest winters.

18. Write the letter of the place that's farthest from the equator.

19. Why is place A hotter than place C?

END OF LESSON 9

A

1

1. cuddly
2. receive
3. shabby
4. princess

2

1. search
2. snuggle
3. tattered
4. velveteen
5. stuffing

3

1. searched
2. received
3. snuggled
4. remembered
5. welcomed
6. stuffed

4

1. shabbier
2. birthday
3. Timmy
4. bunny
5. bunnies
6. months

The Velveteen Rabbit

Retold by José Reyes
Illustrated by Brock Nicol

Timmy was a little boy who had lots of toys, and he liked to play with all of them. But his favorite toy was the velveteen rabbit that he received on his fourth birthday.

Oh, how he loved that soft
cuddly rabbit. At night, he could
not go to sleep unless he snuggled
up with the rabbit close to his body.
When he played out in the yard, he
always had that rabbit with him. He
even talked to his velveteen rabbit.

After a while, the rabbit started to show signs of wear. It became tattered and torn. One of its ears no longer stood up. And its color had changed from a pretty pink color to gray. But Timmy loved it even more than when he had first held it.

Timmy's mother tried to interest Timmy in other toys. She wanted to get rid of the velveteen rabbit because she thought it was dirty and ugly. She said, "Why don't you give me the rabbit, and I'll get you a fine new animal to play with."

"No," Timmy said. "This rabbit is not like the others. This rabbit is real."

"Real?' his mother said. "He's just a toy."

"No," Timmy insisted. "He's real."

The next day, Timmy was playing with the tattered rabbit in the yard when it started to rain. Timmy went inside, but he forgot to take the rabbit with him. When it was time for Timmy to go to bed, he remembered where the rabbit was. He snuck outside in the rain and cold and searched for the rabbit until he found it. Then he hugged his rabbit and said, "You are cold and wet, but I will make you feel better." He took the rabbit inside, dried it, and took it to bed with him. He snuggled up and went to sleep.

A few days later, Timmy became very sick. He had a high fever and strange dreams. In one of his dreams a lovely princess appeared. She said, "The love your rabbit has for you will make you well. And your love for the rabbit will make him real."

Timmy got well, and he remembered what the princess had said. But as the months passed, the poor rabbit became even shabbier than it had been. Part of its stuffing was coming out, and it had a large rip on its back.

One day, Timmy's mother said, "Timmy, you are a big boy now. It's time for you to get rid of that rabbit. It's falling apart."

Timmy said, "But a princess told me that this rabbit will become a real rabbit."

His mother said, "Then why don't you take him out into the woods and leave him there, where he can live with the other rabbits."

Sadly, Timmy agreed. With tears in his eyes, he took his tattered velveteen rabbit to the woods. He put it down in soft leaves, next to a large tree. He patted it and said, "I . . . I have to leave you here . . . but you will be fine. . . . You will be a real rabbit."

He started to walk away, but after he took a few steps he turned around to look at his rabbit for the last time. To his surprise, the tattered rabbit was gone. And sitting in its place was a bunny—a real rabbit.

The bunny hopped over to Timmy and seemed to smile. "Oh," Timmy cried. "You are real." Then the bunny hopped over to where two other bunnies were playing. They welcomed their new friend, and the three of them hopped off.

Timmy often went back into the woods to watch his bunny play with the other rabbits. Although it had changed, Timmy knew that his velveteen rabbit would always love him as much as he loved it.

A

1

1. Inuit
2. son
3. kayak
4. ordinary
5. scientist

2

1. <u>any</u>more
2. <u>day</u>light
3. <u>day</u>time
4. <u>winter</u>time
5. <u>summer</u>time
6. <u>rest</u>less

3

1. January
2. March
3. December
4. February

4

1. grandchild
2. reaches
3. honking
4. friends
5. splashing
6. jacket

5

1. Newnans Lake
2. seventy
3. sir
4. constant
5. ignore
6. spear

6

1. flapped
2. napping
3. kisses
4. tilted

Information About the Tilt of the Earth

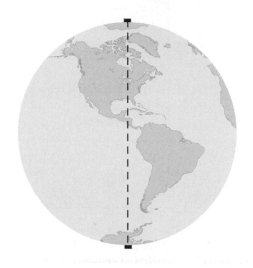

PICTURE 1

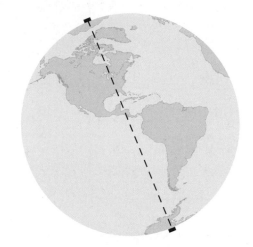

PICTURE 2

The earth is tilted. The poles are not straight up and down. Instead, they tilt. **And the poles tilt the same way as the earth circles the sun.**

Picture 3 shows the tilt of the earth stays the same for all four seasons.

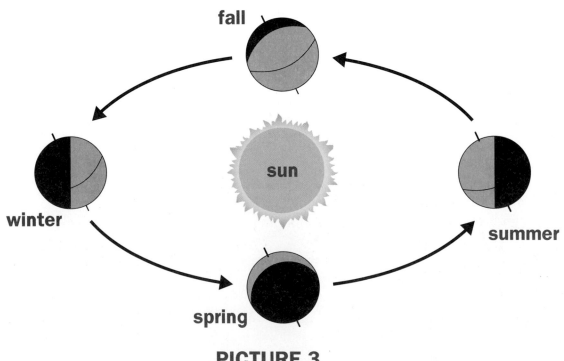

PICTURE 3

Touch the earth at wintertime. **The North Pole tilts away from the sun during winter.** You can see that half of the earth is in shadow and half is in sunlight. But the North Pole is completely in shadow. That means that as the earth spins around and around during wintertime, there is no daylight at the North Pole. There is constant darkness.

Touch the earth at summertime. **The North Pole tilts toward the sun during summer.** Half the earth is in shadow and half is in sunlight.

But the North Pole tilts toward the sun, so it is completely in sunlight. That means that at the North Pole during summer, there is no night. There is daylight all the time during summer. The sun never sets.

Remember: **If the pole tilts away from the sun, it's wintertime at the pole and there is no daylight.**

If the pole tilts toward the sun, it is summertime and there is no night.

C Chapter 10

The Flock Reaches Florida

The next morning before the flock took off, Henry tried out his wing. He took off from the field and flew around the lake. When he landed, Tim came up to him and said, "I know what you were doing. You were trying to see if your wing is all right. Is it?"

"It feels pretty good," Henry said with a smile. "I can fly today."

And he did. The leader of the flock honked out directions to the goose that would be at the point of the V. Then, there were loud splashing and flapping sounds as more than eighty geese took off from Jackson Lake. Tim and Old Henry took their place near the back of the V and the flock went higher and higher.

"Why are we going so high?" Tim asked.

"When we're up high, we'll be able to ride some winds that are blowing toward Florida. We should be able to go far today without doing much work."

The winds blew and the flock flew. Around noon, Henry told Tim, "We're in Florida now."

"Wow," Tim said. "That means we're almost at Crooked Lake."

Henry laughed. "No, we still have a long way to go, and we won't get there today. It's more than two hundred miles to Crooked Lake."

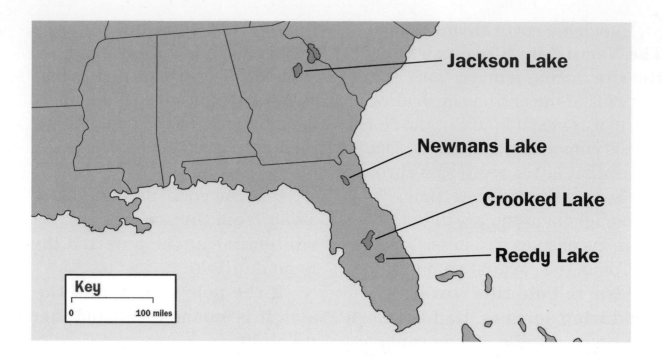

Tim said, "So where will we spend tonight?"

"I don't know. Our flock always stops at Newnans Lake, which is about seventy miles from here. But I don't know where this flock lands."

Less than two hours later, Henry found out where the flock would land—at Newnans Lake.

There were lots and lots of geese around Newnans Lake. ⭐ Tim said, "It looks like all the geese in the world are right here."

"There are a lot of geese here," Henry said. "But wait until you see how many geese there are near Crooked Lake."

The flock circled Newnans Lake and landed near a shore that was covered with geese. Some of them were honking and showing off by flapping their wings. Others were napping. The leader of the flock swam over to Old Henry and said, "We're going to spend tomorrow resting here. Then we'll go to Reedy Lake the next day. Do you plan to fly with us?"

Henry flapped his wings and said, "I do. I feel fine."

Tim smiled and said, "Me, too."

So two days later, Tim and Henry were flying high above Crooked Lake. Henry told Tim, "This is where we leave the flock. Our lake is right down there."

Old Henry flew up near the front of the great V and called to the leader. "Thank you, sir," Henry said. "You're a fine leader and you have a wonderful flock. We were glad to have the chance to fly with you."

"Good luck to both of you," the leader said. Then Henry and Tim swooped down from the flock.

"I can't wait to see my mom and dad," Tim said.

Henry was also looking forward to seeing his old friends and his children and grandchildren. But he also felt a little sad. As the two geese swooped closer and closer to the beautiful blue lake below, Henry knew that he would miss flying with Tim. This trip was the first time in years that Henry felt that somebody really needed his help. That was a good feeling for Henry.

Number your paper from 1 through 16.

D REVIEW ITEMS

1. What's the name of geese that are black, brown, and white?
2. What's the name of geese that are all white?
3. What color are all geese when they are born?
4. Geese live in large groups called ______ .
5. Where are most wild geese born?

6. If you cannot see the sun, it is ______ on your side of the earth.
7. What is it on the other side of the earth?
8. The earth turns around one time every ______ hours.

9. Which letter shows the place that has the warmest winter?

10. Which letter shows the place that is closest to the equator?

11. Which letter shows the place that is closest to a pole?

12. Is the **North Pole** or the **South Pole** closer to that letter?

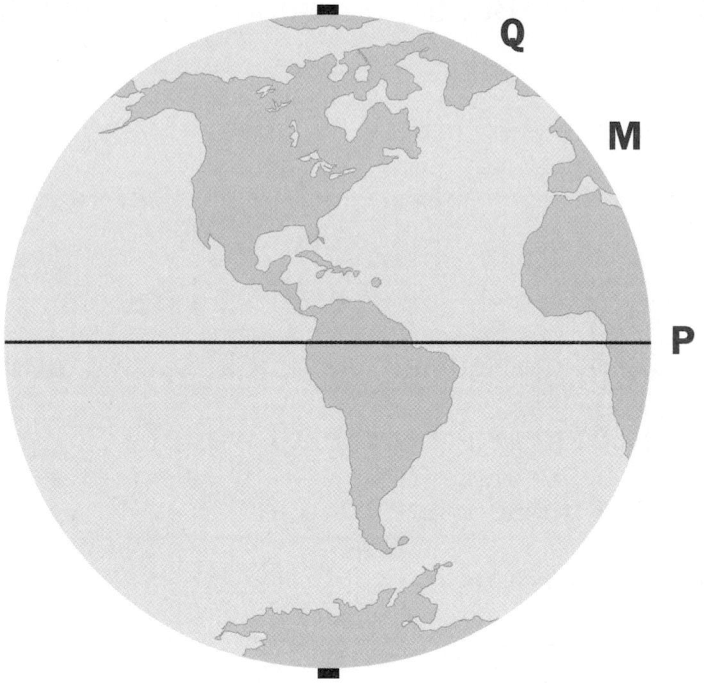

13. The earth makes a circle around the sun one time every ______ .

14. How many days does it take the earth to make one full circle around the sun?

15. Is it easier for a bird to fly alone or with a large flock?

16. Flying near the back of a large flock is like riding your bike ______ .

- with the wind
- against the wind

END OF LESSON 11

A

1
1. polar bear
2. ice floe
3. Oomoo
4. Oolak
5. shoulder
6. wolf

2
1. pebbled
2. splatter
3. Alaskan
4. scattered
5. grandchild
6. midnight

3
1. killer whale
2. Inuit
3. spear
4. January
5. slippery

4
1. parka
2. walrus
3. kayak
4. son
5. restless
6. kisses

Information About Inuits

In the next lesson, you will read about Inuits. The winters are very cold where Inuits live. Inuits live near the North Pole in Canada and Alaska.

Alaska is a state of the United States, but it is far north of the main part of the United States. Touch Alaska on the map.

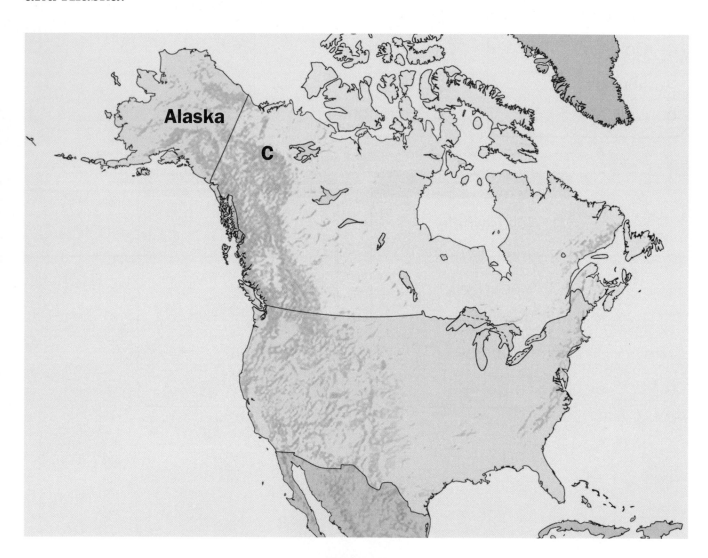

PICTURE 1

Picture 2 shows an Inuit with some of the things that Inuits use.

The Inuit is holding a fishing pole in one hand.

The Inuit is holding a fishing spear in the other hand.

The Inuit is wearing a warm jacket made from animal skins. That jacket is called a parka.

The boat that Inuits use in the summer is called a kayak.

Near the Inuit is a sled. The dogs that pull the sleds are called sled dogs.

Make sure you can read these words:

Inuit	parka	kayak
Alaska	spear	

PICTURE 2

Back to Canada

There were hundreds of geese on Crooked Lake and in the fields around it. Henry and Tim circled the lake twice before Henry spotted their flock. Then he pointed his wing toward the south shore and said, "There's our flock right there."

The two geese flew very low over the flock and honked loudly. As they made a sharp turn and headed back, Henry could hear some of the geese in the flock saying things like, "Who are those geese?" and "Doesn't that one goose look a lot like Henry?"

Tim and Henry landed right in the middle of the flock. Oh, how the geese honked and flapped their wings. Tim's mom flapped her wings so hard she sent little feathers flying all over the place. His dad rushed over and gave Tim a big old goose kiss. "My son," he said, "I didn't think we'd ever see you again."

Tim had tears in his eyes. As Tim ran off with his mom and dad, Henry's friends formed a big circle around him and honked so loudly that you could hear them for miles. A few minutes later, some of his children, grandchildren, and great grandchildren came from their flocks to give Henry big old goose kisses.

One of Henry's grandchildren said, "We didn't think you were coming, but we knew we would see you next summer when we went north again."

"Yes," a great grandchild said, "but now you'll be able to fly back to Canada with us next spring."

Henry started to say, "Oh, I don't know," but then he smiled and said, "Sure. We'll all go back to Canada in the spring."

And that's what happened. Henry spent the winter in the warm Florida sun, napping, eating, swimming, and visiting with his friends and family. About two times every week, he would go flying with some of the geese who were less than a year old. He would always make sure that Tim went with them. ★ Henry would give the young geese practice at flying in a V. Henry would honk out orders as the V would swoop over Crooked Lake very low and very fast. Once in a while, Henry would have a sore wing after flying with the young geese, but his wing wasn't too bad.

Henry wasn't really worried about his wing because the trip back north was a lot easier than the trip down to Florida. The trip north started in January, but the geese wouldn't reach Big Trout Lake in Canada until the middle of April.

At the beginning of January, Tim, Henry, and all the geese began feeling restless. They wanted to fly north. Two days later, the first flocks took off. Over the next few days, Henry watched hundreds and hundreds of flocks take off. Finally, Henry's flock was ready. It flew into the sky and joined other flocks that were leaving Crooked Lake, Reedy Lake, and the other nearby lakes. The geese flew in four great Vs. The sky was filled with geese.

Henry's flock followed the warm weather as it moved north. The flock would stay at a landing place long enough to make sure that the next landing place would not be frozen.

Finally, in the middle of April, the flock arrived at Big Trout Lake. There was honking and flapping as the geese met other flocks that stayed at Big Trout Lake during the summer.

Two days after the flock landed at Big Trout Lake, Tim and Henry said goodbye. It was time for Tim and the other geese that were almost a year old to form their own flock and fly off to Sandy Lake. The

young geese would spend the summer at that lake.

Before Tim left, he gave Henry a big old goose kiss and said, "Thank you for everything you've done. And I hope that I'll see you next winter at Crooked Lake."

Henry said, "I'll be there."

THE END

Number your paper from 1 through 11.

D REVIEW ITEMS

1. When geese learn to fly, do they start in the water or on the land?

2. They run with their ▨▨▨ out to the sides.

3. Which letter shows the part of the earth that receives more heat from the sun than any other letter?

4. Which letter shows a part of the earth that receives less heat from the sun than any other letter?

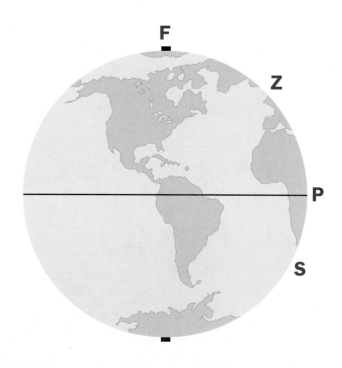

5. The sun shines ▨ .

   • some of the time   • all the time

6. Can you see the sun all day long and all night long?

7. Write the letters of the 2 kinds of places that are safe for geese.

   a. places with many geese

   b. places with a few ducks

   c. places with no geese or ducks

   d. places with a few geese

8. During winter at the North Pole, how much does the sun shine?

   • never   • all the time

9. During summer at the North Pole, how much does the sun shine?

   • never   • all the time

10. What season is it at the North Pole when the North Pole tilts toward the sun?

11. What season is it at the North Pole when the North Pole tilts away from the sun?

A

1

1. hind
2. Alaskan
3. December
4. shoulder
5. nudge
6. icy

2

1. snowball
2. playmate
3. snowdrift
4. slowpoke
5. wherever
6. headfirst

3

1. repeated
2. playful
3. dangerous
4. walruses

4

1. killer whale
2. polar bear
3. ice floe
4. Oolak
5. March

5

1. Usk
2. Oomoo
3. pebbled
4. February
5. scattered

6

1. slippery
2. midnight
3. splat
4. fur
5. wolf

Animals in Alaska

The picture shows some of the animals that live in Alaska. Here are the names of the animals in the picture: polar bear, elephant seal, killer whale, walrus, and wolf.

Tell which animal in the picture is the biggest and which animal is the smallest.

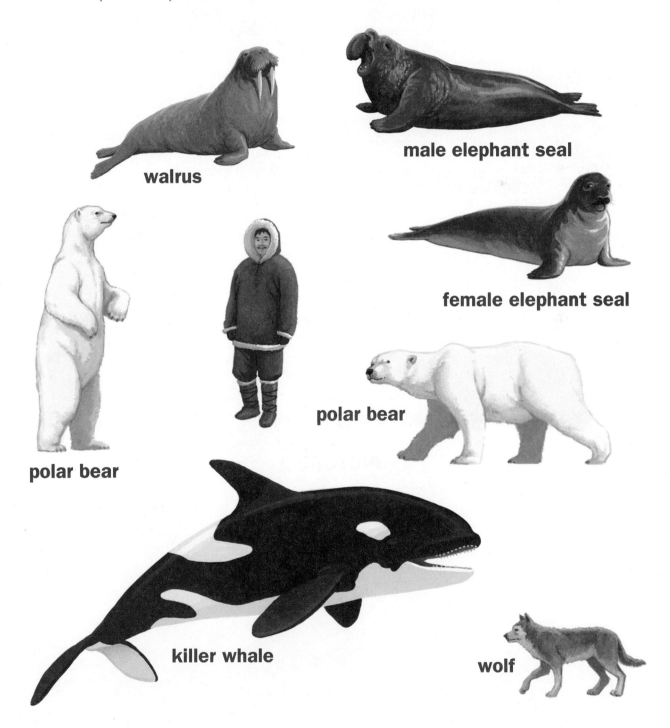

walrus

male elephant seal

female elephant seal

polar bear

polar bear

killer whale

wolf

Where Oomoo and Oolak Lived

In the next story, you will read about Oomoo and Oolak. They were Inuit children who lived in Alaska.

Pictures 1, 2, and 3 show the place where Oomoo and Oolak lived.

PICTURE 1

Pictures 1 and 2 show what their place looked like in the spring. Picture 1 shows how that place looks if you are standing on the beach. Picture 2 shows how that place looks if you are above that place looking down. Picture 2 is like a map of the place. You can see the ice floe in picture 2.

The pebbled beach shows where the sand ends and the ocean begins. Seals are on the pebbled beach, far from the tent. Two walruses are closer on the pebbled beach. Near the end of the ice floe are killer whales.

The tent on top of the hill was Oomoo's summer home.

Picture 3 shows how the same place looked at the end of summer.

Compare the place in spring and at the end of the summer. Tell three things that have changed.

In summer, the seals and the walruses moved away before the water froze. The killer whales also moved away. These animals came back in the spring.

Make sure you can read these words:

seal	walrus	killer whale
ice floe	slope	

PICTURE 2

PICTURE 3

Oomoo and Oolak in Alaska
Oomoo

Oomoo was an Inuit girl who was twelve years old. Oomoo had a brother named Oolak. He was ten. Oomoo and Oolak lived in Alaska, near the ocean. When our story starts, Oomoo and Oolak are very happy. They are happy because it is April. April is a very good time of the year for the Inuits along the Alaskan coast because April is in spring. And in the spring, the days start getting longer and warmer.

In the spring, you can notice the days getting longer. The days get longer because the North Pole of the earth is tilting toward the sun. As the North Pole tilts more and more toward the sun, the days get longer and longer.

If you live in Alaska, the days get very short in the winter and very long in the summer. Look at the picture of the sun and the globes. Globe **W** shows how the earth looks on the first day of winter. The **X** marks the place where Oomoo and Oolak live.

Half of the earth is dark all the time. The place where Oomoo and Oolak live is so close to the North Pole that it is in darkness all winter long.

During Oomoo's winter, there is no daytime. There is only nighttime. That nighttime lasts for weeks and weeks. Imagine not seeing the sun for weeks. Then imagine what it is like to see the sun start coming out for a longer time each day.

Look at globe **S**. It shows the earth on the first day of summer.

You can tell that globe **S** shows the earth during summer because the North Pole is tilting toward the sun. On the first day of summer, it doesn't get dark where Oomoo and Oolak live. They are so close to the North Pole that they can see the sun all the time. For weeks, there is no night—just daytime. ★ Then the sun starts disappearing for a longer time each day.

Remember, in summer the sun shines all the time where Oomoo and

Oolak live. In winter, the sun does not shine at all. If you understand these facts, you can see why Oomoo and Oolak were happy when it was April. During the months of December and January, they had not seen the sun. During the months of February and March, the days got longer and warmer. In April, the days were getting much longer. Now the sun was shining more than 12 hours each day. The little flowers were starting to pop out on hills near the ocean. Thousands of seals were beginning to appear along the shore. Now the days were beautiful. "The sun," Oomoo said to herself and held her hands up. "The beautiful sun." She took a deep breath and smiled at Oolak. He smiled. They were standing on a hill next to the ocean. Tiny white clouds were scattered in the blue sky. The ocean was blue and gray, and it looked very cold. There was still a lot of snow on the ground, but it was wet snow, the kind of snow that made good snowballs.

Oolak made a good snowball. Oomoo figured out what Oolak was going to do, so she started to run away. She ran down the slippery hill and onto the ice chunks. She heard a snowball splat next to her, but she didn't stop. She ran and hollered over her shoulder, "Missed again!" She was smiling as she jumped to the next chunk of ice. She heard another splat next to her.

Then she stopped. In front of her, a huge polar bear was climbing from the water onto the ice. The polar bear was no more than three meters from Oomoo.

Number your paper from 1 through 22.

E STORY ITEMS

1. When days get longer, is the North Pole tilting **toward the sun** or **away from the sun?**

2. When days get shorter, is the North Pole tilting **toward the sun** or **away from the sun?**

3. Oomoo and Oolak might have a hard time going to sleep at night in the summertime. Tell why.

4. In April, the sun shines for more than ▮▮▮▮ hours each day in Alaska.

5. What kind of animal did Oomoo see at the end of the chapter?

6. How far was Oomoo from that animal?

7. During Oomoo's winter, there is no ▮▮▮▮ .

    • daytime   • nighttime

8. Write the letter of the globe that shows how the earth looks on the first day of winter.

9. Write the letter of the globe that shows how the earth looks on the first day of summer.

A

sun

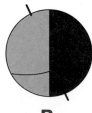
B

10. Write the number of the earth that has the North Pole tilting away from the sun.

11. Write the number of the earth that has the North Pole tilting toward the sun.

12. Write the number of the earth that has darkness all around the North Pole.

13. Write the number of the earth that has daylight all around the North Pole.

Write which season each earth in the picture shows.

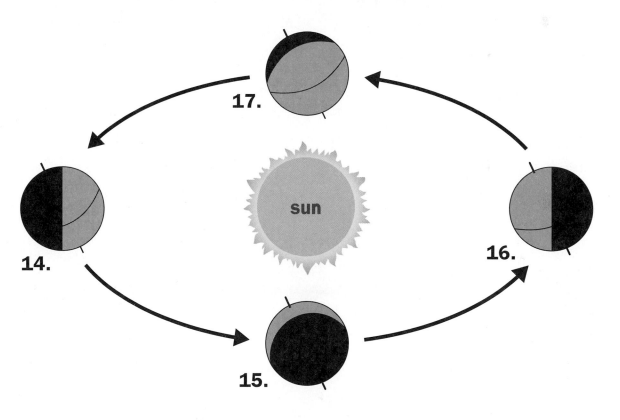

18. How warm is it during winter in Alaska?

19. Which letter on the map shows Alaska?

20. Which letter shows Canada?

21. Which letter shows the main part of the United States?

22. Which 2 letters show where Inuits live?

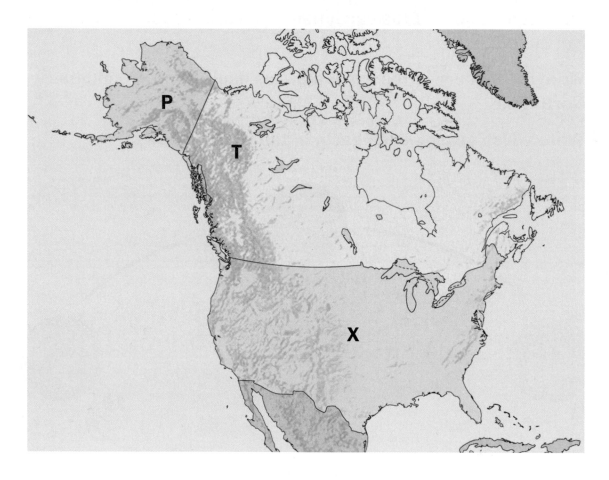

A

1
1. collar
2. remain
3. orca
4. headfirst
5. numbered
6. wherever

2
1. nudged
2. scrambled
3. growling
4. tossing
5. playmate
6. dogsled

3
1. tumbling
2. hitch
3. ridge
4. hind
5. fur
6. icy

4
1. snowdrifts
2. dangerous
3. slowpoke
4. repeated
5. playful

Information About the Dangerous Season

The animals in Alaska are most dangerous in the spring. The male animals are ready to fight anything, and the females have babies in the spring. After they have had babies, they will fight any animal that bothers their babies.

Other dangerous animals in Alaska are polar bears, wolves, and walruses. The picture shows two animals fighting on the beach.

The winner of the fight will keep his place on the beach, and the loser will have to find another spot on the beach. Wherever the loser goes, he will probably have to fight another seal.

Remember, these animals are most dangerous in the spring.

Usk the Polar Bear

"Usk," Oomoo shouted. "Usk, you big hill of white. Where have you been?"

The huge polar bear stood up and wagged his head from side to side. He was nearly three meters tall when he stood up on his hind legs. Oomoo started to run toward Usk, but then she stopped. She remembered what her father had told her last fall, when the days were starting to get short. Her father had told her that Usk was no longer a bear cub. He was a full-grown bear and full-grown bears are not pets.

Now Oolak was standing on the ice chunk next to Oomoo. "Wow," he said, "Usk has grown a lot since last fall."

"Yes," Oomoo said. "Usk is beautiful." She was right. Usk's coat was white-white, so bright in the sun that the color hurt Oomoo's eyes.

As she looked at Usk, she remembered the first time she had ever seen him. Hunters had shot Usk's mother three years ago. Usk was just a baby, no bigger than a puppy. When Oomoo found Usk, he was very skinny and he could hardly move. For months she fed him milk

from a bottle that she had made out of animal skins. Usk grew bigger and bigger. He became the best playmate that anybody ever had. He loved to run and wrestle in the snow. He slid down steep snowdrifts headfirst. He slid down them tail first. In fact, he would sometimes slide down them as he turned around and around, with his legs sticking out in all directions as he swept a wide path down the snowdrift.

✿ As Oomoo stood near the great bear, she found it hard to believe that this same bear used to fit inside her parka or that this bear used to sleep on the floor of her winter home.

Usk had been Oomoo's friend for over two years, but last fall something about him changed. ★ He still liked to play sometimes, but at other times he didn't seem to be interested in Oomoo or in being with her. Usk would go off by himself and walk along the high slopes, sometimes howling into the air like a dog. Sometimes he wouldn't come down to see Oomoo for three or four days at a time. And each time ✿ he came back, he didn't seem as playful as he had been the time before.

One day late in the fall, another polar bear came over the hills. It was a young male, about the same size as Usk. Usk attacked that bear and drove it away. That was the day that Oomoo's father told her and Oolak not to go near the bear anymore. "Usk is a bear," her father had told them. "And bears do what bears do. They are not pets. Do not go near Usk anymore. He could hurt you."

Oomoo stood there on the ice chunk, looking up at Usk. She remembered what her father had told her.

Oomoo wanted to run over and give that great big bear a great big hug. She wanted to bury her face in his heavy white fur. She wanted to slide down the slopes with him. But she just stood there, smiling. "Hi, Usk," she said. Her brother repeated the greeting.

Usk dropped to all four legs and lowered his rear end, the way he always did when he wanted to play.

"Usk wants to play," Oolak hollered. Oolak was holding a wet snowball. He threw it at Usk and hit the bear in the shoulder. "Come on, Usk," he yelled, and ran back toward the shore.

Oomoo was going to remind her brother that they should not play with Usk. But before she could say anything, the bear bumped into her, almost knocking her into the icy water. Usk ran past her after Oolak, who was running toward the beach and hollering, "Here I am, you big white slowpoke."

Oomoo started running after the bear. She began to laugh.

D **REVIEW ITEMS**

Choose from these words to answer each item:

- Canada
- Florida
- sun
- equator
- migration
- poles
- moon
- geese

1. The heat that the earth receives comes from the ▮▮▮▮ .

2. The part of the earth that receives more heat than any other part is the ▮▮▮▮ .

3. The parts of the earth that receive less heat than any other part are called the ▮▮▮▮ .

Write the name of each numbered object in the picture. Choose from these names:

- fishing pole
- spear
- parka
- sled dogs
- sled
- kayak

10. When days get longer, is the North Pole tilting **toward the sun** or **away from the sun?**

11. When days get shorter, is the North Pole tilting **toward the sun** or **away from the sun?**

12. In April, the sun shines for more than ____ hours each day in Alaska.

13. Which globe shows how the earth looks on the first day of winter?

14. Which globe shows how the earth looks on the first day of summer?

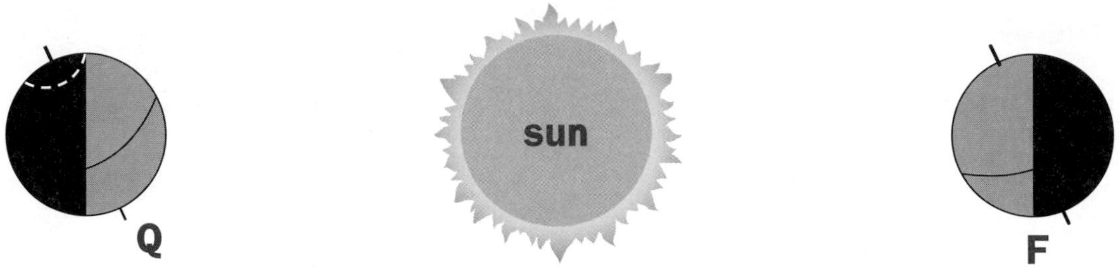

15. What kind of boat do Inuits use in the summer?

16. Why don't they use those boats in winter?

END OF LESSON 14

A

1
1. mosquito
2. actually
3. punish
4. no-see-ums
5. area
6. marine

2
1. speckled
2. nudged
3. scrambled
4. sliced
5. stamped

3
1. forth
2. cliff
3. ignore
4. hitch
5. scientists
6. ordinary
7. orca

4
1. swarming
2. sloshing
3. growling
4. tumbling
5. sledding

5
1. key
2. collar
3. enter
4. careless
5. dogsled
6. remain

Information About Florida, Canada, and Alaska

You've read about places in Florida, Canada, and Alaska. See what information you remember about those places.

- Which place in Canada did you read about?
- Who lived there?
- Who lived in Alaska?
- Which place is farthest south, Florida, Big Trout Lake, or Alaska?
- Which place is farthest north?

- Which place has the warmest winters?
- Which place has the coldest winters?

Here's a map that shows Canada and Alaska.

You can see the route that goes from Big Trout Lake to where Oomoo and Oolak lived. Use the key to figure out about how far it is between these two places.

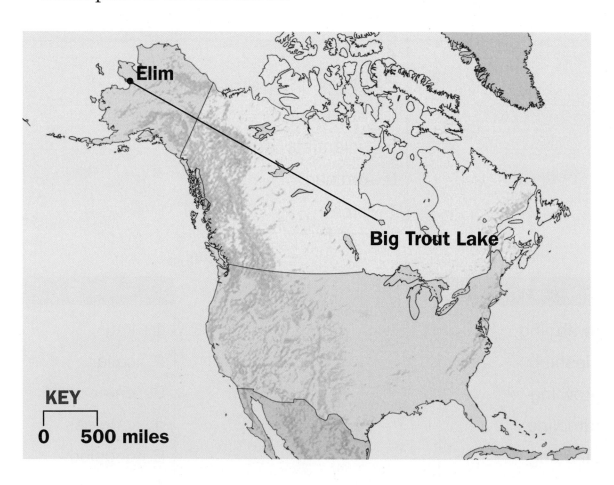

KEY

0   500 miles

Playing with Usk

Oolak ran very fast, but Usk ran even faster. Usk caught up to Oolak just as Oolak reached the beach. Usk nudged Oolak with his nose, and Oolak went tumbling in the pebbles.

Usk made a growling sound and shook his head, but Oomoo knew that he was just playing the way dogs sometimes do. Oolak got to his feet and started to stumble through the pebbles. Before he got two meters down the beach, however, Usk caught up to him again, gave him a nudge in the back, and down went Oolak.

Oomoo ran to the edge of the beach where there was a snowdrift that was about a meter deep. She made a snowball and threw it at Usk. Splat! It hit him on the rear end. He turned around and stood up.

Usk made a growling sound and chased Oomoo. He caught up to her, grabbed her by the collar, and pushed her over. She went face first into the snowdrift next to the pebbled beach.

She rolled over and laughed. Usk was sitting in the snow next to her, panting. With his big pink tongue hanging out, he looked like a great big white dog. She tossed some snow at his tongue. He licked his chops, and then started to pant again.

"Hey," Oolak said. "Let's hitch him up to the sled."

Oomoo remembered the fun that she and Oolak used to have sledding down the hills with Usk. She used to hitch him to their dogsled and let him run down the hills. Sometimes he would stop halfway down and the sled would run into him. Then everybody would tumble down the hill. Sometimes he would run very fast and then make a turn at the bottom of the hill. The sled would slide in a great circle and then turn over, tossing Oomoo and Oolak into the snow.

Sometimes Usk would . . .

"Oomoo," her father shouted.

Oomoo stopped thinking of sledding with Usk and looked up on the top of the hill, where her father was standing. "Oomoo," he shouted again. "Oolak, come here now." Oomoo and Oolak scrambled up the slope through the wet snow.

The top of the hill was free of snow. Oomoo stamped the snow from her feet and looked down. She did not want to look at her father. She could feel that he was looking at her.

"Oomoo, I am ashamed of you," he said. "What season of the year is it?" Oomoo answered quietly.

Her father said, "And in what season are bears the most dangerous?"

"Spring," she said.

"And what did I tell you about playing with Usk?"

Oomoo replied, "We should not go near him."

Her father said, "If you cannot stay away from that bear, you will have to stay where he will not go."

D   SKILL ITEMS

Here are three events that happened in this chapter:

    a. Her father said, "And in what season are bears the most dangerous?"

    b. Oolak got to his feet and started to stumble through the pebbles.

    c. With his big pink tongue hanging out, he looked like a great big white dog.

1.   Write the letter of the event that happened near the beginning of this chapter.

2.   Write the letter of the event that happened near the middle of this chapter.

3.   Write the letter of the event that happened near the end of this chapter.

Use the words in the box to write complete sentences.

ignore	splat	route	swimmers	ordinary
playful	scientists	restless	constant	

4.   The horses became ▩ on the dangerous ▩ .

5.   ▩ do not ▩ ▩ things.

E   REVIEW ITEMS

6.   In which direction do geese fly in the fall?

7.   What is this trip called?

8.   The earth is shaped like a ▩ .

9. The hottest part of the earth is called the ▨ .

    • pole   • desert   • equator

10. The ▨s are the coldest places on the earth and the ▨ is the hottest place on the earth.

11. How many poles are there?

12. The farther you go from the equator, the ▨ you get.

    • colder   • fatter   • hotter

---

13. At which letter would the winters be very, very cold?

14. At which letter would the winters be very, very hot?

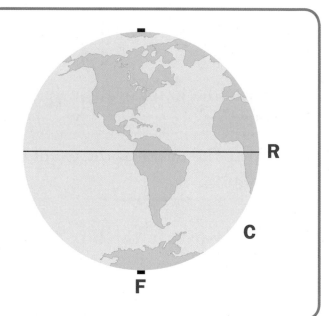

---

15. Is it easier to fly alone or with a large flock?

16. Flying near the back of a large flock is like riding your bike ▨ .

    • with the wind   • against the wind

17. What season is it at the North Pole when the North Pole tilts toward the sun?

18. What season is it at the North Pole when the North Pole tilts away from the sun?

19. In what season are animals most dangerous in Alaska?

20. During what season do female animals in Alaska have babies?

END OF LESSON 15

A

1
1. numb
2. shrank
3. sliced
4. itch
5. remain

2
1. grinding
2. glanced
3. swarming
4. speckled
5. feeding

3
1. groans
2. creaks
3. mosquitoes
4. no-see-ums
5. orcas
6. marine

4
1. punished
2. punishment
3. sloshing
4. forth
5. schoolyard
6. area

B Passage 1

Information About Killer Whales

You'll be reading more about killer whales. Here are facts about killer whales:

- Killer whales are about 24 feet long. Most other whales are much longer than killer whales.
- Killer whales are not fish. Fish are cold-blooded. Whales are warm-blooded, like bears, humans, and dogs.
- Killer whales are very smart. Some scientists think that killer whales are smarter than dogs.
- Killer whales hunt in packs. They kill larger whales, polar bears, seals, or any other animal that is in the water.

More Information About Killer Whales

Another name for a killer whale is orca.

Orcas are warm-blooded animals. Groups of orcas hunt in packs. Orcas feed on fish, birds, seals, bears, and any other animals in the water. Members of a pack often work together to catch a meal. Pack members sometimes force many fish into a small area and then take turns feeding on them.

Sometimes part of the pack swims onto the land to scare seals. The seals jump into the water to escape, but other orcas are waiting for them.

Orcas are among the fastest marine animals; they are able to swim at more than 35 miles per hour!

Baby orcas are born in the fall. They weigh 400 pounds and may be as long as seven feet. A baby will remain with its mother for at least two years.

The Beach

Oomoo's father said, "You must stay away from Usk."

Then he ordered Oomoo and Oolak to stay near their summer home for two full days. Oomoo and Oolak were not to go down to the beach or on the ice floe or into the hills. Oomoo's family had just moved into their summer home, which was a tent on a ridge near the ocean.

Their winter home was in a valley, where the hills helped protect them from the screaming winter winds. The summer home was much smaller but nicer than the winter home. It was made from animal skins. The only problem with the summer home was the bugs.

As soon as the snow starts to melt in Alaska, insects come out. Mosquitoes come out in clouds—millions and millions of them. The mosquitoes don't seem to bother the bears or the dogs, but they sure bother humans. There are also biting flies in Alaska. Biting flies look like ordinary flies, but they bite like mosquitoes. They leave red bumps that itch.

There are other biting flies—very small ones. And there are also little insects so small that you have to look very carefully to see them. They come out when the sun goes down, and they bite. Their bites feel like mosquito bites, but they do not leave a red mark. These tiny bugs are called no-see-ums.

Oomoo didn't like the bugs, but she managed to ignore them most of the time. And Oomoo's summer home was in a place where the wind blew hard. When the wind blew, the bugs stayed away.

Oomoo was being punished, but she really didn't mind sitting there on the hill near her summer home, looking down at the beach. ★ The beach was like a circus that had a million different acts. There were acts from the elephant seals. They were swarming on the beach about half a mile from Oomoo's summer home. Male seals were fighting for the best places on the beach.

Closer to Oomoo was another act. Two walruses were lying on a part of the beach that was speckled with thousands of birds. In the ocean were the killer whales, swimming back and forth just beyond the end of the ice floe. The killer whales were waiting for the seals to enter the water.

As Oomoo watched the killer whales, she remembered a time when she had been very close to them. She had been out in a kayak with her father. It was late spring and the ocean was very calm. Oomoo's father paddled the kayak past the end of the ice floe. Suddenly, three huge killer whales appeared in the water. The fins of the killer whales sliced through the water as they circled the boat. Then one of the whales lifted its head out of the water and seemed to look right at Oomoo. The whale opened its mouth and Oomoo could see the shiny white row of knives. The whale was only a few meters from the kayak. It looked at Oomoo for a few seconds, then slipped back into the water, making a sloshing sound. Oomoo and her father sat silently in the kayak. Oomoo was so frightened that her hands were shaking. Then slowly, the three killer whales moved away from the kayak.

As Oomoo sat on the ridge looking out at the killer whales and thinking about what had happened, she could feel goose bumps on her arms. "I never want to be that close to killer whales again," she said to herself. Then the sounds on the beach caught her attention. Some of the birds near the two walruses were fighting.

Number your paper from 1 through 13.

E REVIEW ITEMS

1. Female animals fight in the spring to protect ▆▆▆ .

2. Name 2 kinds of Alaskan animals that are dangerous in the spring.

Write the name of each animal in the picture.

3.

4.

6.

5.

7.

8.

9. Which animal in the picture is the biggest?

10. Which animal is the smallest?

11. The map shows a route. What state is at the north end of the route?

12. What country is at the south end of the route?

13. About how many miles is the route?

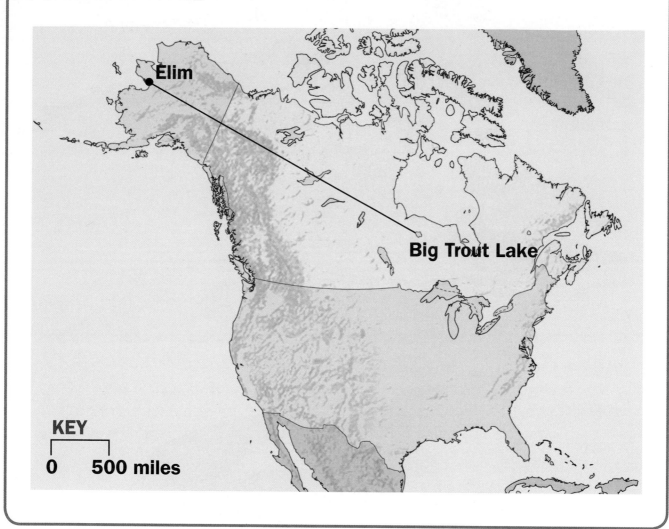

KEY

0   500 miles

A

1
1. surface
2. current
3. careless
4. schoolyard
5. punishment

2
1. creaks
2. buzzes
3. floes
4. moans
5. groans
6. sheets

3
1. melting
2. glanced
3. shrank
4. numb
5. drifting
6. grinding

B Chapter 5

The Ice Floe

Ice floes melt in the spring. During the winter, parts of the ocean are covered with very thick ice. In some places, the ice is three meters thick. During the winter, you can walk far out on the frozen ocean. Then the spring comes and ice starts to melt. When it melts, chunks of ice break off and float into the ocean. Some of these chunks are as big as a schoolyard. Some are no bigger than a table.

When an ice floe begins to break up in the spring, you can hear it. At night, as you lie in your summer home, you can hear many sounds. You can hear the sound of wolves and sometimes bears growling. You can hear a million buzzes from a million bugs that circle above you. You can hear the occasional bark of the seals. And you can hear the ice floe. It moans and groans. It creaks and it cracks. Sometimes, it squeaks and squeals. It's a sound that you'll never forget and that you learn to love.

Ice floes also make noise in the winter. The ice floes creak and groan when the air is so cold that sweat freezes to your face. The air is so cold that a deep breath hurts and makes you cough.

In the winter, the ice floes creak and groan because great sheets of ice are crowding together and there is not enough room for them. So the ice floes buckle. Sometimes great chunks of ice break off and are pushed over other chunks. The chunks make noise when they move around.

But the sound that the ice chunks make in the spring is different. Now the chunks are melting and sliding back into the water. To Oomoo, the chunks sounded happy in the spring. They seemed to say, "I'm free to float into the ocean."

Oomoo loved to play on the ice chunks in the spring, but she knew that she had to be careful and follow the rule. The rule was that she could never go out to the chunks near the end of the ice floe. That was where the killer whales were.

During the spring there was always a small pack of whales waiting in the water just beyond the end of the ice floe. ★

Here's why it was very dangerous to be on the ice chunks near the end of the ice floe. If the ice chunk that you were standing on drifted out into the ocean, you could not get back. Someone would have to save you. But you would be very far from shore—maybe more than a mile. Maybe the people from your village would not hear your calls for help. If they didn't, the chunk of ice would float farther and farther into the ocean. Then it would melt. It would get smaller and smaller. As it shrank, the killer whales would move closer and closer to the ice chunk. But even if the killer whales didn't attack you, you would die within minutes after you went into the water. The water is so cold that it would take only a few minutes for your arms and legs to become so numb that you could not move.

• • •

Oomoo's punishment was over. She had just finished lunch. She could see her breath as she ran along the pebbled beach. She listened to the grinding sound of the pebbles under her feet. "Here's a good one," Oolak shouted. He was on the ice floe, pointing to a chunk of ice that was right in front of him. The chunk was a perfect size. It was about four meters across. Oomoo ran over to her brother. Then they jumped onto the ice chunk. The ice chunk rocked a little bit when they landed on it.

The ice floe was shaped like a giant letter C. The ice chunk that Oomoo and Oolak were on was near the bottom end of the C. Oolak pointed across the water to a place on the other side of the C. He said, "The ice chunk will drift over there. Then we can walk back."

For a moment, Oomoo was going to say, "That's a pretty long

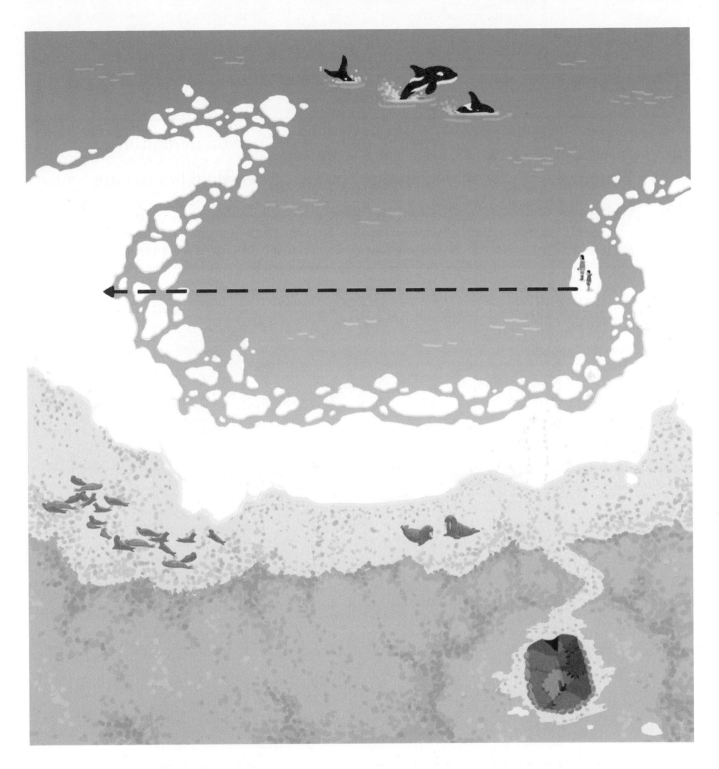

way to drift." Then she turned around and faced the wind. It was blowing from the east. If it kept on blowing, it would move the ice chunk to the place Oolak pointed to.

She glanced at the killer whales just beyond the end of the ice floe. Then she said, "Okay, let's go." The ice chunk had already drifted a few meters.

C REVIEW ITEMS

1. Write the letter of the earth that shows the person in daytime.

2. Write the letter of the earth that shows the person 6 hours later.

3. Write the letter that shows the person another 6 hours later.

4. Write the letter that shows the person another 6 hours later.

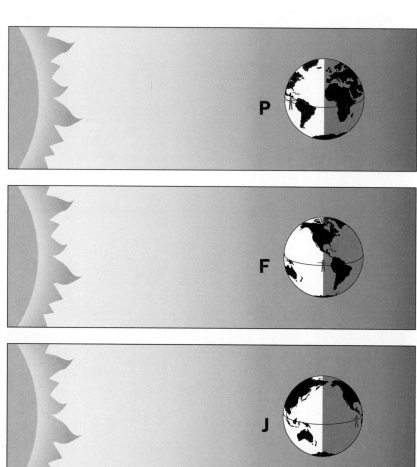

5. Which letter on the map shows Alaska?

6. Which letter shows Canada?

7. Which letter shows the main part of the United States?

8. Which 2 letters show where Inuits live?

9. How warm is it during winter in Alaska?

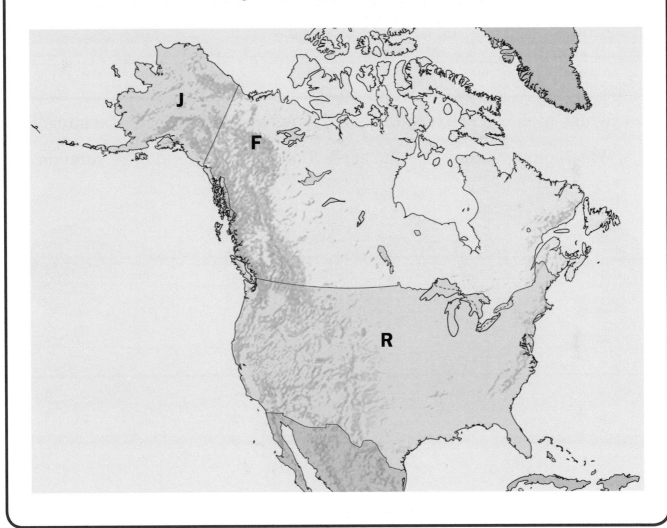

10. About how long are killer whales?

11. Compare the size of killer whales with the size of other whales.

12. Are killer whales fish?

13. Tell if killer whales are **warm-blooded** or **cold-blooded.**

14. Name 3 animals that are warm-blooded.

15. Name 3 animals that are cold-blooded.

16. Which globe shows how the earth looks on the first day of winter?

17. Which globe shows how the earth looks on the first day of summer?

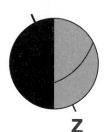

Z

sun

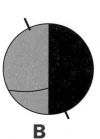

B

A

1
1. gripping
2. careless
3. stung
4. surface
5. current

2
1. destroyed
2. posts
3. whistling
4. drowned

B

Information About Drifting

You're reading about an ice chunk that is drifting. Here is a fact about how things drift in the ocean:

- Winds make things drift.

If the wind blows hard, the wind will push things and make them move. The wind will make things move in the same direction the wind blows. The picture shows wind blowing a cloud. Which direction is that wind coming from?

Here is another fact about how things drift in the ocean:

- Ocean currents also make things drift.

Ocean currents are like great rivers of water within the ocean. An ocean current moves. If you are in an ocean current, you will move in the same direction the current moves.

The picture shows two ocean currents, A and B. In which direction is ocean current A moving?

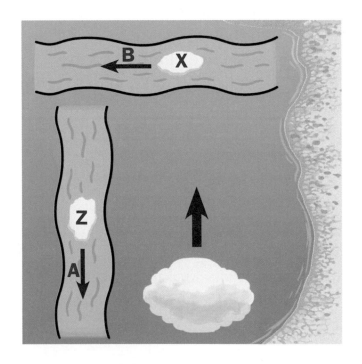

In which direction is ocean current B moving?

Remember the facts about how things drift. Winds make things drift. Currents make things drift. Something in a wind moves in the direction the wind is moving. Something in a current moves in the direction the current is moving.

Drifting on an Ice Chunk

The sun felt very warm as Oomoo and Oolak stood on the drifting chunk of ice. The flies and mosquitoes were thick near the shore, but when the ice drifted into the open water, the insects were not as thick. Soon there were very few insects bothering Oomoo and her brother. Slowly, the ice drifted west, toward the other side of the C-shaped ice floe.

"Let's rock the ice," Oolak said, and began to jump up and down on one end of the ice chunk. Oomoo moved next to him and began to jump at the same time that Oolak jumped.

The ice began to rock more and more, making waves and a great sloshing sound. The cold ocean water swirled and jumped, sometimes coming over the surface of the ice.

Oomoo was looking at the water, careful not to get too close to the edge of the ice chunk. She did not want to fall into the ocean. Suddenly, she noticed that the water turned dark—from a sparkling blue to a purple, and her shoulders were no longer warm. Everything looked darker.

She looked south to see the sun, but it was behind a cloud. The cloud was not the kind of cloud you see when the weather is nice. It was a low storm cloud, a fat cloud that had a bottom layer that looked almost green.

Oomoo knew about these clouds. Her father and the other men of the village had told many stories of the green clouds and how they brought winds that could sweep a boat out into the ocean. The men of the village told that anybody going into the ocean should look at the sky—always look at the sky. Oomoo knew that as soon as you spotted a green cloud, you should get to shore immediately. Even if that

cloud seemed to be many miles away, you should not wait. ★ The cloud would move in very fast, and when it did, it would bring terrible winds and rain. Oomoo had seen green clouds before. Once they came and almost destroyed Oomoo's tent. The winds blew so hard that they knocked down the strong posts that held up the tent. Oomoo remembered that she and Oolak stretched out on the tent and held on to the tent posts as hard as they could. If they had tried to stand up, the wind would have blown the tent into the ocean.

Oomoo remembered those things. But as she looked up at the great cloud that had covered the sun, she realized that she and Oolak had been careless. They hadn't followed the rule about watching the sky.

Suddenly, the wind tore across the ocean like a great rake. The wind made a dark path as it raced across the surface of the water. The water was smooth in front of the place where the wind touched down. Where the wind hit the water, the surface was rough with sprays of water blowing into the air.

"That wind will blow us north into the open water," Oomoo shouted. "Get down, Oolak, and find something to hang on to."

Oomoo and Oolak got down and watched the wind moving from the shore. The wait seemed very long, but it was only a few seconds. The wind was moving about 40 miles per hour.

Suddenly, the wind hit them. With a whistling sound, it hit. Oomoo held on with one hand over the edge of the ice chunk. She stuck the other one in a hole on the surface of the chunk. The spray of the water hit them. More wind. More spray. Now bigger waves, blowing and washing over the top of the ice chunk. The water was icy, and the wind was blowing. The ice chunk was drifting straight north, out into the ocean.

Number your paper from 1 through 19.

D **SKILL ITEMS**

She actually repeated that careless mistake.

1. What word means **to do something again?**

2. What word means the opposite of **careful?**

3. What word means **really?**

Here are three events that happened in the chapter:
  a. The wind tore across the ocean like a great rake.

  b. And the cloud was not the kind of cloud you see when the weather is nice.

  c. Soon there were very few insects bothering Oomoo and her brother.

4. Write the letter of the event that happened near the beginning of the chapter.

5. Write the letter of the event that happened near the middle of the chapter.

6. Write the letter of the event that happened near the end of the chapter.

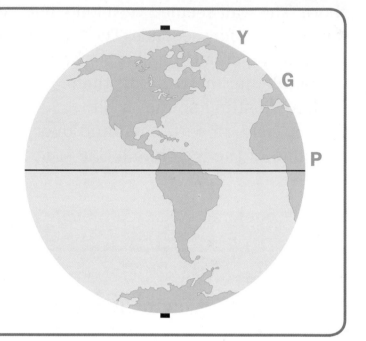

7. Which letter shows the place that has the warmest winters?

8. Which letter shows the place that is closest to the equator?

9. Which letter shows the place that is closest to a pole?

10. Is the North Pole or the South Pole closer to that letter?

11. The earth makes a circle around the sun one time every ▮▮▮▮ .

12. How many days does it take the earth to make one full circle around the sun?

13. When days get longer, is the North Pole tilting toward the sun or away from the sun?

14. When days get shorter, is the North Pole tilting toward the sun or away from the sun?

15. In April, the sun shines for more than ▮▮▮▮ hours each day in Alaska.

16. During which season do ice floes start to melt?

17. During winter in Alaska, you can walk far out on the ocean. Tell why.

18. Do ice floes make noise in the winter?

19. Why do ice floes make noise in the spring?

END OF LESSON 18

A

1
1. kneeled
2. hailstone
3. gripping
4. drowned
5. playfully

2
1. actually
2. stung
3. marble
4. dents

B Chapter 7

The Storm

If the wind hadn't started to blow, Oomoo and Oolak would have drifted west to the other side of the C-shaped ice floe. But the wind blew them off course. The wind was blowing from the shore, directly from the south. The wind blew everything north. The last place in the world that Oomoo and Oolak wanted to go was north. Oomoo noticed that the ice chunk was already very close to the end of the ice floe. Once the ice chunk went past the ice floe, there were currents that would take it farther and farther into the ocean, where it would melt.

"Help! Help!" Oomoo shouted, but her voice was small against the sounds of the wind.

The wind howled. It whistled. It made great blowing sounds. And it threw water so hard that the drops stung when they hit. "Help!" Oomoo shouted.

The waves were crashing over the side of the chunk now, almost washing Oomoo into the ocean. She tried to keep her face turned toward shore. "Help!" she hollered.

Suddenly, she heard Oolak's voice behind her. It was almost drowned out by the sound of the wind. "Oomoo," he called. She turned around and looked at the ice chunk. But she couldn't see Oolak. He had been washed into the water. Then she saw his hands. They were gripping the top edge of the ice chunk.

She slid over and looked down into the water. "I can't get up," he shouted.

She rolled on to her back and let her feet hang over the side of the ice chunk. "Grab my legs," she shouted.

PICTURE 1

He grabbed her legs. He started to climb up, but when he did, he almost pulled Oomoo into the water with him. She started to slide, and she probably would have slid into the water if that big wave hadn't hit the ice chunk. ★

That wave hit the shore side of the ice chunk. It lifted up the shore side and then pushed it very hard. The wave actually slid the ice chunk right under Oomoo and Oolak. In fact, it turned the chunk and moved it so fast that Oomoo and Oolak ended up right in the middle of the chunk.

PICTURE 2

PICTURE 3

✿ Oolak looked very frightened and cold. His eyes were wide. Oomoo tried to hold on to him and keep him from slipping off. "Are we going to die?" he shouted.

"No, we're okay," Oomoo said. She was lying. She didn't see any way that she and Oolak could survive.

Then suddenly the wind died. The waves still rolled and continued to push the ice chunk beyond the floe. But the big wind had stopped. Rain and hail started to fall. The rain and hail made more noise than the wind had made. "Help!" Oomoo shouted. But she was starting to lose her voice.

"Let's shout together," she said to Oolak. "One, two, three: help! ✿ They repeated the shout again and again, until they could not yell anymore. Still the rain and the hail pounded down. Even though the rain was cold, it was much warmer than the ocean water.

After half an hour, the rain began to die down. When the rain had been coming down very hard, Oomoo had not been able to see more than a few meters. Now she could see where they were. The ice chunk was near the top of the C-shaped ice floe and it was still moving north. Oomoo looked to the ocean, past the ice floe, and she could see them—five or six of them. Sometimes they would roll out of the water so that she could see the black-and-white marking around their heads. Sometimes they would move along with only their fins above the water. Oomoo saw the killer whales but she didn't say anything to Oolak.

Number your paper from 1 through 20.

C SKILL ITEMS

Use the words in the box to write complete sentences you have learned.

ordinary	repeated	enter	scientists	ignore
careless	numb	actually	hitch	

1. ____ do not ____ ____ things.
2. She ____ ____ that ____ mistake.

Here are three events that happened in the chapter:

a. Oomoo noticed that the ice chunk was very close to the end of the ice floe.

b. Sometimes they would roll out of the water so that she could see the black-and-white markings around their heads.

c. Just as Oomoo was sliding off, a huge wave hit the shore side of the ice chunk.

3. Write the letter of the event that happened near the beginning of the chapter.
4. Write the letter of the event that happened near the middle of the chapter.
5. Write the letter of the event that happened near the end of the chapter.

6. Name 2 things that can make an ice chunk drift.

7. In which direction will you drift when you're in an ocean current?

8. In which direction will you drift when you're in a strong wind?

9. What kind of boat do Inuits use in the summer?

10. Why don't they use those boats in the winter?

11. Write the number of the earth that has the North Pole tilting away from the sun.

12. Write the number of the earth that has the North Pole tilting toward the sun.

13. Write the number of the earth that has darkness all around the North Pole.

14. Write the number of the earth that has daylight all around the North Pole.

Write which season each earth in the picture shows.

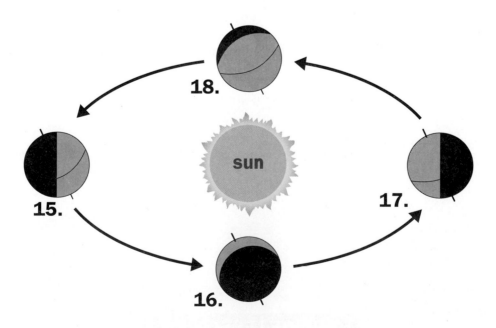

19. During winter at the North Pole, how much does the sun shine?

   - never   • all the time

20. During summer at the North Pole, how much does the sun shine?

   - never   • all the time

A

1
1. material
2. whether
3. barren
4. comet
5. literature
6. attract

2
1. winged
2. outrunning
3. smoother
4. swifter

3
1. fiction
2. nonfiction
3. rocket
4. spinning
5. heavens

B

Literature Types

There are different types of literature. Some literature is **fiction.** This is material that is made up and did not really happen. Fiction is false. It is make-believe.

The other type of literature is **nonfiction.** Nonfiction literature is true. It tells about real people or things.

There are different kinds of fiction. Whether the literature is true or not, it can be presented in many forms. Those forms are stories, drama (or plays), and poetry.

Dreams

By Langston Hughes
Illustrated by Alva Lind

Hold fast to dreams
For if dreams die
Life is a broken-winged bird
That cannot fly.

Hold fast to dreams
For when dreams go
Life is a barren field
Frozen with snow.

The Runner

By Faustin Charles
Illustrated by Gabhor Utomo

Run, run, runner man,
As fast as you can,
Faster than the speed of light,
Smoother than a bird in flight.
Run, run, runner man,
No one can catch the runner man,
Swifter than an arrow,
Outrunning his own shadow.
Run, run, runner man,
Faster than tomorrow.
Run, run, runner man,
Quicker than a rocket!
Into deep space spinning a comet!
Run, run, runner man,
Lighting the heavens of the night,
Run, run, runner man,
Out of sight,
Run, run, runner man, run!

A

1

1. mukluks
2. wrist
3. hailstone
4. playfully
5. thunderstorm
6. waterdrop

2

1. droplets
2. spanking
3. straps
4. tangled

3

1. gulped
2. gently
3. owed
4. wavy
5. kneeled
6. dents

4

1. rose
2. sight
3. marble
4. dove

Information About Clouds and Water

You have read about a big storm cloud. Here is information about clouds:

- Clouds are made up of tiny drops of water.

- In clouds that are very high, the waterdrops are frozen. Here is how those clouds look.

PICTURE 1

- Some kinds of clouds may bring days of bad weather. These are low, flat clouds that look like bumpy blankets.

PICTURE 2

- Some clouds are storm clouds. They are flat on the bottom, but they go up very high. Sometimes they are five miles high.

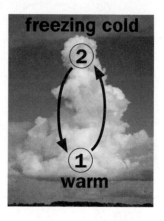

PICTURE 3

The arrows in picture 3 show how the winds move inside a storm cloud. The winds move waterdrops to the top of the cloud, where the drops freeze. When a drop freezes, it becomes a tiny hailstone. The tiny hailstone falls to the bottom of the cloud, where the tiny hailstone gets covered with more water. Then it goes up again and freezes again. Now the hailstone is a little bigger. It keeps going around and around in the cloud until it gets so heavy that it falls from the cloud. Sometimes it is as big as a baseball; sometimes it is smaller than a marble.

If you want to see how many times a hailstone has gone to the top of the cloud, break the hailstone in half. You'll see rings. Each ring shows one trip to the top of the cloud. Count the rings and you'll know how many times the hailstone went through the cloud. Hailstone A went through the cloud three times.

How many times did hailstone B go through the cloud?

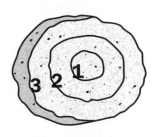

HAILSTONE A

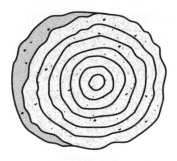

HAILSTONE B

C Passage 2

How Clouds Form and Move

Clouds are made up of very tiny drops of water or specks of ice. The drops are so small and light that they can float in the air.

When air rises, it cools. Cool air can't hold as much water as warm air, so millions and millions of these droplets come together and form a white cloud that you can see.

Clouds move with the wind. High clouds are pushed along by winds that move at more than 100 miles per hour. When clouds are part of a thunderstorm, they usually travel at only 30 to 40 miles per hour.

The Killer Whales Wait

Oomoo took off one of her boots. She kneeled down and slammed the boot against the surface of the ice. The boot made a loud spanking sound. Oolak watched for a moment, then took off one of his boots and slapped it against the surface of the ice. "Maybe they'll hear this," Oomoo said. "I hope they do," she added, but she knew that it was still raining a little bit and that the rain made noise. She also knew that she and Oolak were far from shore—too far. They were more than a mile from the tent. She guessed that the sounds they made with their boots were lost in the rain and the slight breeze that was still blowing from the south.

From time to time, Oomoo glanced to the ocean. She hoped that she would see the killer whales moving far away. She hoped that the sound of the boots would scare them away. But each time she looked in their direction, she saw them moving back and forth, just past the top of the C-shaped ice floe.

Suddenly, Oolak tugged on Oomoo's shoulder and pointed toward the whales. His eyes were wide and he looked as if he was ready to cry. "I know," Oomoo said. Her voice was almost a whisper. "Just keep trying to signal," she said. "Maybe the people on the shore will hear us."

As she pounded her boot against the surface of the ice, she stared toward the shore. She wanted to see a kayak moving silently through the rain, or hear the signal of a bell ringing. She wanted to…

Suddenly, she saw something white moving through the water. At first, she thought that it was a chunk of ice. But no, it couldn't be. It was not moving the way ice moves. It was very hard to tell what it was through the light rain. It wasn't a kayak or a long boat. It was … Usk.

Usk was swimming directly toward the ice chunk, and he was moving very fast. ★

"Usk!" Oomoo yelled as loudly as she could. "Usk!" She stood up and waved her arms.

The huge polar bear caught up to the ice chunk when it was not more than a hundred meters away from the killer whales. "Will they go after Usk?" Oolak asked.

"They'll go after Usk if they're hungry," Oomoo replied. "We've got to get out of here fast."

The huge bear swam up to the ice chunk, put his huge paws on the surface, and started to climb onto it. When he tried that, he almost tipped it over.

"No, stay down," Oomoo said, as she tried to push him back. He rolled into the water and made a playful circle. "Give me your laces," Oomoo said to Oolak. Oomoo and Oolak untied the laces from their boots. These laces were long, thick straps made of animal skin. Oomoo tied all the laces together and quickly glanced back. The ice chunk was less than a hundred meters from the killer whales.

She called Usk. He playfully swam around the ice chunk, rolling over on his back and slapping the water with his front paws. Oomoo waited until Usk got close to the shore side of the ice chunk, and then she slipped the laces around his neck. "Hang on tight," she told Oolak, and handed him one end of

the laces. She and Oolak sat down on the ice chunk and tried to dig their heels into dents in the surface of the ice.

"Play sled," she told Usk. "Play sled. Go home."

At first, Usk just rolled over and almost got the laces tangled in his front paws. "Home," Oomoo repeated. "Play sled and go home."

Usk stayed next to the ice chunk, making a playful sound. "Home," Oomoo shouted again.

Then Usk seemed to figure out what he was supposed to do. Perhaps he saw the fins of the killer whales and perhaps he didn't. But he got low in the water and started to swim toward shore.

Number your paper from 1 through 13.

E STORY ITEMS

1. What were Oomoo's boot laces made of?

2. What did Oomoo do with the laces after she tied them together?

3. What did she want Usk to do?

4. Did Usk immediately understand what he was supposed to do?

5. What did Usk start doing at the end of the story?

F SKILL ITEM

Mukluks

Hunters near the North Pole move quietly and quickly in their <u>mukluks</u>. They do not weigh very much, but they keep feet warm and dry. People of all ages wear them.

6. What are mukluks?

    • fur hats   • warm boots   • parkas   • gloves

G REVIEW ITEMS

7. Female animals fight in the spring to protect ▬▬ .

8. Name 2 kinds of Alaskan animals that are dangerous in the spring.

9. Is it easier to fly alone or with a large flock?

10. Flying near the back of a large flock is like riding your bike ▬▬ .

    • with the wind   • against the wind

11. The map shows a route. What state is at the north end of the route?

12. What country is at the south end of the route?

13. About how many miles is the route?

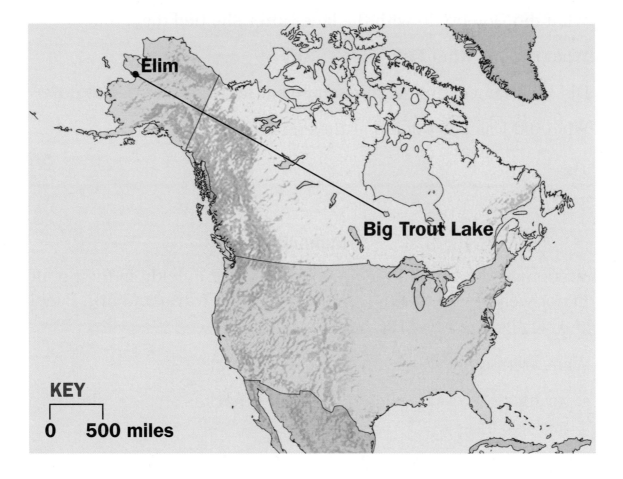

A

1

1. Mesozoic
2. dinosaur
3. Triceratops
4. skeleton
5. Tyrannosaurus
6. explode

2

1. earlier
2. mukluks
3. wavy
4. gently

3

1. figure
2. sight
3. rose
4. dove
5. wrist

4

1. smoked
2. leaned
3. gulped
4. owed
5. pricked

Piles

Here's a rule about piles:
Things closer to the bottom of the pile went into the pile earlier.

Here's a pile:

Which thing is closest to the bottom of the pile?

So is that the thing that went into the pile first? Did the shoe go into the pile before the bone went into the pile?

Look at the cup and the bone. Which object is closer to the bottom of the pile? So which object went into the pile earlier?

Look at the pencil and the rock. Which object is closer to the bottom of the pile? So which object went into the pile earlier?

The rule tells us that things closer to the bottom of the pile went into the pile earlier. Use this rule to figure out which object was the **last** one to go into the pile.

Use the rule to figure out which object went into the pile just after the shoe went into the pile.

Use the rule to figure out which object went into the pile just after the pencil went into the pile.

Usk and the Killer Whale

When Usk began to swim toward shore, he moved with so much power that he almost pulled Oomoo and Oolak off the ice. They leaned back and dug their heels in. They hung on to the laces as hard as they could hang on.

Oomoo looked over her shoulder. She saw a terrible sight. One of the fins was moving toward them. The fin rose out of the water, and she could see that the whale was looking at them. Its mouth was open and she could see the row of knives in its mouth. She clearly saw the wavy black-and-white markings on its body. Then it dove into the water.

Its fin disappeared. But the whale was moving very fast.

Quickly, Oomoo tied the laces around her wrist so that she had a free hand. With that hand, she slapped the ice. "Maybe this sound will scare it off," she said to herself. "Oh, please go away," she said out loud. "Please."

She looked into the water and suddenly she saw the huge form of the whale pass under them. Her heart was pounding so hard that she seemed to shake all over. She kept looking down, but she didn't see anything for about a minute. Then she saw the whale roll out of the water about five meters in front of them.

The bear made a growling sound and pricked up his ears. For a moment, Usk stopped swimming. Then he continued.

"Oh, please go away," Oomoo repeated to herself. Again, the form of the great whale moved under them, making a slight turn to the right. Oomoo continued to slap the ice with her hand. Oolak was saying something, but Oomoo couldn't think about that. She thought about one thing—that whale.

Suddenly, the whale rolled out of the water behind them. It seemed to be turning away, toward the other whales. "Please go away," Oomoo said. Usk swam, Oomoo and Oolak held on to the laces. And Oomoo kept looking behind to see what the whale would do next. ★ Suddenly, she saw it roll out of the water again. It was more than sixty meters from them. That whale was moving toward the other whales.

•　•　•

The mosquitoes were terrible. So were the biting flies. There was no breeze at all, and the bugs were thick. But Oomoo didn't mind. She and Oolak had to stay near the tent. Oomoo and Oolak couldn't go on the slopes or down the path to the beach. They couldn't play. Their father had told them they had to study the sky and the ocean so they would not make the kind of mistake they made before.

"When you look at the sky," their father had told them, "face into the wind and look at the place where the sky meets the land or the ocean."

The day was peaceful, with the wind blowing gently from the ocean. Oomoo watched the sky and the ocean. From time to time, she looked at the killer whales. She wondered what that whale had thought, and why it hadn't attacked Usk. "You will never understand the whale," an old man of the village had told her.

That afternoon, everyone in the village gathered at Oomoo's tent. The people formed a great ring. They sang. Then Oomoo's father led Usk into the middle of the ring. Women brought him a large smoked fish— his favorite food. He gulped it down and wagged his head from side to side. Then Oomoo's father took blue paint and painted the outline of a whale on each side of Usk.

"Let this bear live under the sign of the whale," her father said. "Let no hunter shoot this bear or bother this bear. If this bear needs food, feed this bear. We owe much to this bear. Let us thank him."

The people from the village cheered and danced. Oomoo and Oolak danced with the others. They were very, very proud of their bear. They knew that they should not play with him because he was a bear, not a playmate. But they also knew that they owed their lives to that huge, white, playful bear.

THE END

Number your paper from 1 through 17.

---

1. Things closer to the bottom of the pile went into the pile ▭ .

Look at the pile in the picture.

2. Which object went into the pile **first?**

3. Which object went into the pile **last?**

Write the name of each animal in the picture.

4.

5.

6.

7.

8.

9.

10. Which animal in the picture is the biggest?

11. Which animal in the picture is the smallest?

12. About how long are killer whales?

13. Compare the size of killer whales with the size of other whales.

14. What are clouds made of?

15. What kind of cloud does the picture show?

16. What happens to a drop of water at **B**?

17. The picture shows half a hailstone. How many times did the stone go through a cloud?

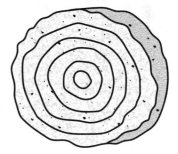

A

1
1. Atlantic Ocean
2. Bermuda Triangle
3. Andros Island
4. Africa
5. engineer
6. prepare
7. volcano

2
1. armor
2. dinosaur
3. layers
4. Tyrannosaurus
5. skeleton
6. explode

3
1. earliest
2. Triceratops
3. killers
4. Mesozoic
5. explaining

B

Layers of the Earth

You learned a rule about piles. Which things went into the pile earlier? We use the rule about piles to figure out how things happened a long time ago.

Look at picture 1. It shows a large cliff. There are rows of stones and rocks and seashells. Each row is called a layer. The layers are piled up. That means the layers closer to the bottom of the pile came earlier.

Which layer went into the pile earlier, layer C or layer D?

Some of the dinosaurs were much bigger than elephants; other dinosaurs had great spikes on their tails. No dinosaurs are alive today. The only place we find their bones is

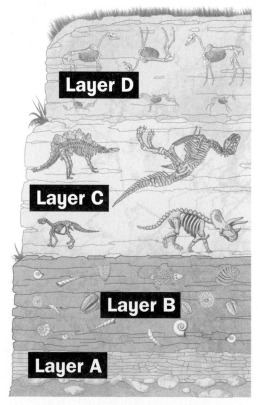

PICTURE 1

in layer C. We can't find dinosaur bones in layer B, and we can't find them in layer D.

When we look at the layers of rock, we find skeletons of animals and shells of animals. In layer B, we find strange fish and other animals that lived many millions of years ago. In layer D we find the skeletons of horses. Near the bottom of layer D, we find horses that are no bigger than dogs. Near the top of layer D, we find horses that are as big as the horses of today.

When we look at layer C, we find the skeletons of some very strange animals. These are dinosaurs. ★

The layers of rock tell us a great deal about things that happened millions and millions of years ago. They tell us what it was like when the great dinosaurs walked on the earth. There were no horses, bears, elephants, or rabbits. There were no mice or cats, but there were many animals. Most of them were probably cold-blooded animals.

Some dinosaurs ate big animals. These dinosaurs were huge killers that could move fast. The ones that are found near the top of layer C stood almost twenty feet tall.

When we move above layer C, we find the beginning of animals that we know—horses, cats, bears, pigs. No layers show skeletons of humans, but if human skeletons were in the picture, they would be at the very top of the pile, in layer D.

Here's another fact about the layers: When we dig a hole in any part of the world, we find the same layers. If we dig a hole in Africa or in Canada, we find skeletons of elephants near the top of the pile. We find dinosaurs in the next layer down.

The layer that has dinosaur skeletons is called the Mesozoic. The layer that came after the Mesozoic is the top layer, which has no skeletons of dinosaurs. This layer is still being laid down. We live at the top of the top layer and we walk on the top layer.

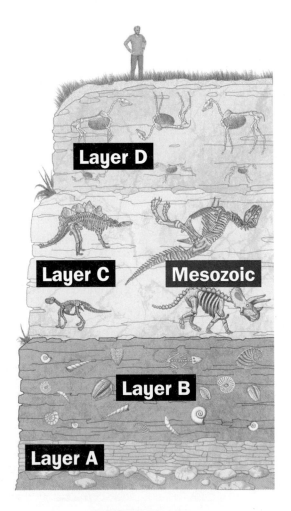

PICTURE 2

C SKILL ITEMS

The smell attracted flies immediately.

1. What word means **right now?**

2. What word means **really interested** the flies?

D REVIEW ITEMS

3. The sun shines ▭ .

   • some of the time   • all of the time

4. Can you see the sun all day long and all night long?

5. If you can see the sun, is it **daytime** or **nighttime** on your side of the earth?

6. What is it on the other side of the earth?

7. The earth turns around one time every ▭ hours.

8. How many heat lines are hitting place **X** on the map?

9. Write the letter of the place that's the coldest.

10. Why is place **T** hotter than place **X?**

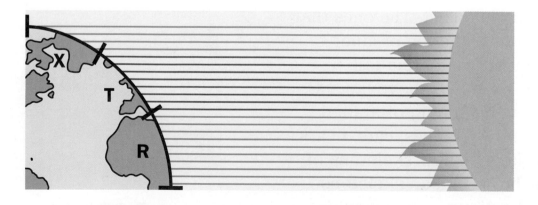

11. Which object went into the pile first?

12. Which object went into the pile **last?**

13. Which object went into the pile **earlier,** the bone or the book?

14. Which object went into the pile **earlier,** the shoe or the bone?

15. Which object went into the pile **just after** the book?

16. Which object went into the pile **just after** the bone?

17. Things closer to the bottom of the pile went into the pile ▭ .

18. Write the letter of the storm clouds.

19. Write the letter of the clouds that may stay in the sky for days at a time.

20. Write the letter of the clouds that have frozen drops of water.

A

B

C

END OF LESSON 23

A

1	2	3
1. <u>Florida</u>	1. Andros Island	1. Mesozoic
2. <u>stormy</u>	2. Bermuda Triangle	2. armor
3. <u>warning</u>	3. Atlantic Ocean	3. Triceratops
4. <u>Carla</u>	4. Edna Parker	4. Tyrannosaurus
5. <u>pre</u>pare	5. volcano	5. exciting
6. <u>ex</u>plaining		6. squawking

B

Dinosaurs of the Mesozoic

You've read about the Mesozoic. What kind of animals lived in the Mesozoic? The picture shows two of the most important dinosaurs that lived in the Mesozoic.

The huge killer dinosaur that lived late in the Mesozoic is named Tyrannosaurus. Tyrannosaurus was about twenty feet tall, which is twice as tall as an elephant. The dinosaur with the horns and the armor is named Triceratops. Tyrannosaurus did not have an easy time killing Triceratops.

Edna and Carla's Adventure
Edna Parker

Edna Parker was thirteen years old. She had been out on her father's ship before. But this was the first time that her father, Captain Parker, let Edna bring a friend along.

This was going to be a great trip for Edna. On other trips, Edna had a problem. She became bored. There was never anything for her to do on the ship after it left the harbor. Sometimes she would sweep up or help with the meals, but most of the time she just sat around and looked over the side of the ship at the swirling water. With Carla along, Edna would have fun.

• • •

✿ Captain Parker was explaining the trip to the two girls. He pointed to a map of Florida and the Atlantic Ocean as he spoke.

"We are starting from here," he said, pointing to the tip of Florida. "We are going to follow this dotted line to an island called Andros Island." Captain Parker continued, "That means we will pass through a place where hundreds of ships have sunk or been lost. It's called the Bermuda Triangle." Captain Parker continued, "Many sailors say the Bermuda Triangle is the most dangerous part of the ocean."

Carla's face seemed to drop.

"Hey," Captain Parker said, and smiled. "Nothing's going to happen in a big ship like this. We ✿ are very safe. ★ And this is not the stormy season."

Carla asked, "Why is the Bermuda Triangle such a dangerous part of the ocean?"

"Bad seas," the captain answered. "There are huge waves and storms that come up without any warning. And there are whirlpools."

Edna said, "You know what whirlpools are, don't you, Carla?"

"I think I know what they are," Carla replied.

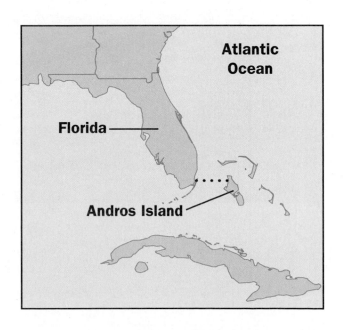

Captain Parker said, "Let me explain. Did you ever watch water that was going down the drain? Sometimes it spins around and around and it makes the shape of an ice cream cone."

"I've seen those," Carla replied. "They suck water right down the drain."

"Yes," Captain Parker said. "Those are tiny whirlpools. The kind of whirlpools that you find in the Bermuda Triangle are just like those, except they are big enough to suck a ship down."

"Wow," Carla said.

Edna was trying to imagine a huge whirlpool.

Captain Parker said, "Well, girls, Andros Island is only 120 miles from here, so we should arrive there in less than a day. We should have a smooth trip. The weather looks good. I am going to look over some maps now. You girls may play on deck, but stay away from the sides of the ship. And stay away from the lifeboats."

"All right, Dad," Edna said, and the girls rushed onto the deck.

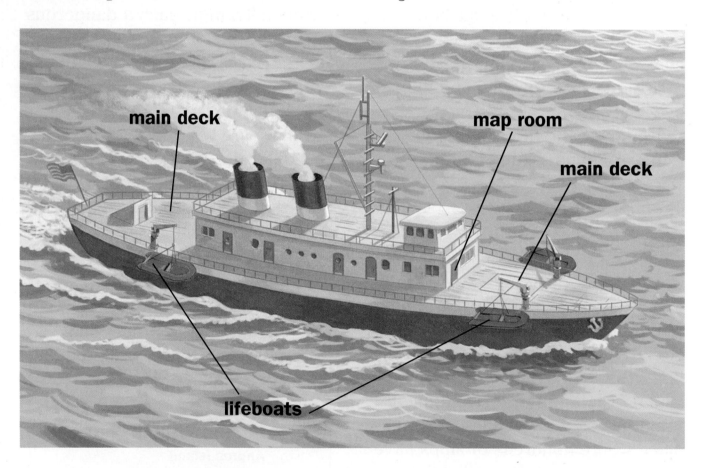

main deck

map room

main deck

lifeboats

D INFORMATION ITEMS

Use these names to answer the questions:

Tyrannosaurus, Triceratops.

1. What is animal A?
2. What is animal B?

A   B

E SKILL ITEMS

Use the words in the box to write a complete sentence you've learned.

immediately   restless   repeated   actually   laughed

attracted   careless   ordinary   gently

3. She ▨ ▨ that ▨ mistake.
4. The smell ▨ flies ▨ .

Look at the map.

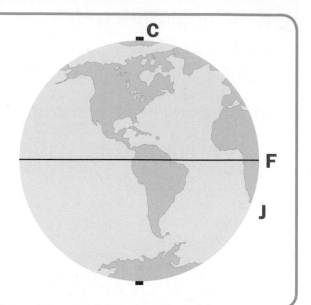

5. What's the name of the place shown by the letter C?

6. Which letter shows the coldest place?

7. Which letter shows the hottest place?

8. Which letter is farthest from the equator?

9. During which season do ice floes start to melt?

10. During winter in Alaska, you can walk far out on the ocean. Tell why.

11. What kind of boats do Inuits use in the summer?

12. Why don't they use those boats in the winter?

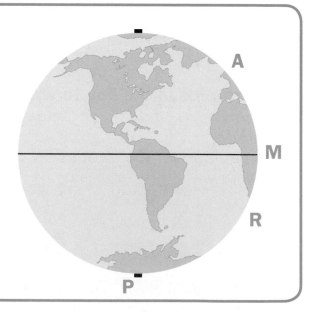

13. Which letter shows the part of the earth that receives more heat from the sun than any other part?

14. Which letter shows the part of the earth that receives less heat from the sun than any other part?

15. Which came **earlier** on the earth, dinosaurs or horses?

16. Which came **earlier** on the earth, strange sea animals or dinosaurs?

17. Write the letter of the layer that went into the pile **first.**

18. Write the letter of the layer that went into the pile **next.**

19. Write the letter of the layer that went into the pile **last.**

20. Which layer went into the pile **earlier,** B or D?

21. Which layer went into the pile **earlier,** A or D?

22. Write the letter of the layer where we would find the skeletons of humans.

23. Write the letter of the layer that has dinosaur skeletons.

24. Write the letter of the layer where we would find the skeletons of horses.

25. Write the letter of the layer we live on.

26. What's the name of layer C?

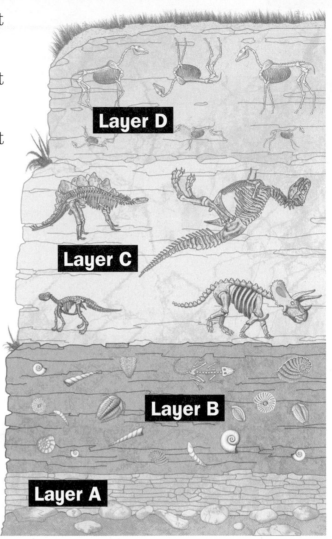

PICTURE 1

27. What kind of animals lived in the Mesozoic?

A

1

1. seagulls
2. elevator
3. surface
4. pirates
5. instant
6. handkerchief

2

1. first mate
2. mast
3. engineer
4. silent
5. dashed
6. beads

3

1. galley
2. stern
3. touch
4. pretend
5. roughed

4

1. exciting
2. powered
3. squawking
4. sliced

5

1. hailstone
2. spyglass
3. tiptoe
4. schoolroom

Looking for Something to Do

Edna and Carla had dashed out of the map room. They had run to the stern of the ship, where they watched the seagulls that followed the ship. The girls watched the waves roll off the stern of the ship.

Then the girls ran to the galley. The cook was busy. They tried to talk to him, but the only thing he wanted to talk about was how much his new gold tooth hurt. After the girls spent about five minutes in the galley, they went to the engine room.

The engine room in a ship is the place where the ship's engine is. Some ships have engines that are as big as a schoolroom. The engine of Captain Parker's ship was not that big. It was about the size of a small truck.

The engineer looked at the girls and said, "What do you think you're doing here?"

They told him that they were looking around. He replied, "If you want to stay here, I'll put you to work. So if you don't want to work, get out."

The girls left the engine room. They walked around the front deck. They thought about climbing the ladder that went up to the top of the mast. But that seemed too scary.

At last the girls sat down on the front deck near a lifeboat. They sat and they sat and they sat. The girls tried to talk about different things. Edna studied the water. Then she realized that she was doing the same kinds of things that she used to do when she went alone on these trips. She was sitting in the sun watching the water.

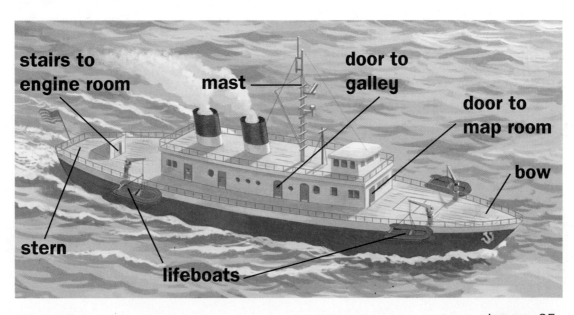

stairs to engine room

mast

door to galley

door to map room

bow

stern

lifeboats

The sea was very calm, like a sheet of glass. The ship sliced through the water and left waves that moved out in a giant **V** as far as Edna could see.

There were beads of sweat on Carla's forehead. Carla said, "This Bermuda Triangle isn't as exciting as they say it is."

Edna nodded. "Yeah, this is boring."

For a moment, the girls were silent. Edna heard the squawking sound of the seagulls and the steady hum of the great engine that powered the ship. Then Carla said, "I wish we had our own boat. Then we could have some fun. I could be captain and you would be my first mate."

The girls looked at each other and smiled. Edna said, "Why don't we pretend that we have our own ship?"

Carla said, "I see a boat we can use for our game." She pointed to a lifeboat that was hanging at the side of the ship. It was ready to be lowered into the water in case of trouble.

Edna shook her head no. She said, "Remember what my dad told us? Stay away from the lifeboats."

"Oh, come on, Edna. We won't get in trouble if we are careful. We won't

touch anything. We'll just sneak into the lifeboat and play for a while."

"No," Edna said slowly, looking at the lifeboat. Edna hadn't made up her mind to do it, but she looked around to see if any of the crew members could see them. She was just trying to figure out how hard it would be to sneak into the boat. No crew members were in sight.

"Come on," Carla said with a big smile. "Come on, Edna. The coast is clear."

Number your paper from 1 through 27.

C SKILL ITEMS

Write the word from the box that means the same thing as the underlined part of each sentence.

they'd	spices	center	leaning
we'd	discovered	throne	hay

1. They put the table in the <u>middle</u> of the room.

2. The horses came running to get some <u>dried grass</u>.

3. <u>We would</u> rather play a game.

D REVIEW ITEMS

Use these names to answer the questions:

Tyrannosaurus, Triceratops.

4. What is animal K?

5. What is animal L?

K

L

6. Captain Parker's ship passed through a place where hundreds of ships have sunk or been lost. Name that place.

7. Write the letters of the 3 things you find in the Bermuda Triangle.

   a. streams   c. huge waves   e. ice floes

   b. sudden storms   d. whirlpools   f. mountains

8. When geese learn to fly, do they start in the water or on land?

9. They run with their ▮▮▮▮ out to the side.

10. What's the name of the line that goes around the fattest part of the earth?

11. What's the name of the spot that's at the top of the earth?

12. What's the name of the spot that's at the bottom of the earth?

Choose from these words to answer each item:

- moon
- Florida
- sun
- equator
- geese
- poles
- Canada
- migration

13. The heat that the earth receives comes from the ▮▮▮▮ .

14. The part of the earth that receives more heat than any other part is the ▮▮▮▮ .

15. The parts of the earth that receive less heat than any other part are called the ▮▮▮▮ .

---

16. Write the letters of the 2 kinds of places that are safe for geese.

   a. places with a few geese   c. places with many geese

   b. places with a few ducks   d. places with no geese or ducks

Write the name of each numbered object in the picture. Choose from these names:

- kayak
- spear
- parka
- fishing pole
- sled
- sled dogs
- mukluks

24. Do ice floes make noise in the winter?

25. Why do ice floes make noise in the spring?

26. In which direction will you drift when you're in an ocean current?

27. In which direction will you drift when you're in a strong wind?

END OF LESSON 25

A

1
1. exhibit
2. displayed
3. mysterious
4. bailed
5. hoping

2
1. shallow
2. tearing
3. hind
4. practice
5. bow

3
1. spyglass
2. surface
3. instant
4. besides
5. lightning

4
1. elevator
2. forty
3. handkerchief
4. perhaps

5
1. bailing
2. roughed
3. glassy
4. tiptoed
5. pirates
6. sloshed

B   Chapter 3

The Lifeboat

Carla and Edna were on the deck of Captain Parker's ship. Carla pretended to take out her spyglass and look around. "We're on an island," she said. "And there's our boat, pulled up on the beach." She pointed to the lifeboat. "I'm the captain and you're my first mate. So when I give you an order, you carry it out."

Edna pulled off her shoes and socks and rolled up her pants to the knees. She tied a handkerchief around her head. She felt like a sailor now. "Yes sir, Captain, sir," she said as she stood up. The deck felt very hot on Edna's feet.

"Remember, we're on an island," Carla said. "We have to be very careful when we sneak into our boat. There are pirates on this island. Follow me."

Carla crouched down and tiptoed across the deck to the lifeboat. She climbed in the front and said softly, "The coast is clear."

"Ouch, ouch, ouch," Edna whispered as she tiptoed across the deck. Edna jumped into the lifeboat, which rocked from side to side. It was held in the air by ropes that were attached to the bow and to the stern. Edna knew that you could do something with the ropes to lower the boat into the water, but she wasn't sure how to do it—and she didn't want to find out.

For a moment, Edna had a bad feeling because they were doing something they shouldn't do. But then Edna explained things to herself. There wasn't anything else to do; none of the crew members would talk to them; and besides, the girls would be very careful.

As Edna turned around, the boat suddenly dropped. Carla must have grabbed one of the ropes at the front of the boat or perhaps the rope just slipped. Edna didn't know. All she knew was that the boat was falling like a high-speed elevator. The ropes were making a howling sound as they ran through the wheels that had been holding the lifeboat. Edna

wanted to yell something, but her voice wouldn't work.

The bow of the boat hit the water before the stern. Edna held on to the side of the boat as hard as she could, but when the boat hit the water, Edna went flying forward, bumping into Carla. A huge wave broke over the front of the lifeboat and sloshed around in the bottom of the boat. ★ Then the boat bounced through the waves that the large ship was making. A huge wave broke over the side of the boat. For an instant, Edna was amazed at how loud the waves were. From the deck the ocean had seemed almost silent. But now there were rushing sounds, splashing sounds, sloshing sounds, and roaring sounds. The waves from the stern of the big ship hit the lifeboat and almost turned it over.

Carla tried to stand up. She was waving her arms and yelling. Edna yelled, too. "Help!" "Stop!" "Here we are!" they yelled. The girls waved their arms. They continued to wave as the large ship became smaller, smaller, smaller. Then the girls stopped waving and continued to watch the large ship which was now only a dot on the glassy water.

Suddenly, as the girls watched the dot, a very cool breeze hit them from behind. The air suddenly had a different smell, and the wind roughed up the surface of the water.

Edna turned around and looked up. Behind the lifeboat was a great storm cloud that rose up and up. "Oh no," Edna said. Then her mind started to work fast. She noticed how deep the water was in the bottom of the boat. "Let's get our life jackets on and start bailing the water out of this boat. We're in for a storm."

When the girls started bailing, there was about 8 inches of water in the bottom of the boat. The girls bailed and bailed, but the waves got bigger and bigger. Now there was only about 3 inches of water in the boat, but the waves hitting the boat were very big and they were starting to splash over the side. The girls bailed and bailed and the waves splashed and splashed. Now there was about 4 inches of water in the boat.

The girls had to stop bailing when a terrible wind hit the boat and almost knocked them over. The waves were so large that Edna had to hang on to the side of the boat. She just kept hanging on and hoping that the storm would stop. But the waves were now over twenty feet high and the winds were moving forty miles per hour. The boat was going up and down the waves.

Number your paper from 1 through 19.

C INFORMATION ITEMS

Here are three events that happened in the chapter.

Write **beginning, middle,** or **end** for each event.

1. The girls had to stop bailing when a terrible wind hit the boat.

2. The ropes were making a howling sound as they ran through the wheels that had been holding the lifeboat.

3. Carla pretended to take out her spyglass and look around.

D REVIEW ITEMS

4. In which direction do geese fly in the fall?

5. What is this trip called?

6. Geese live in large groups called ▨ .

7. Where are most wild geese born?

A   B   C

8. Write the letter of the clouds that may stay in the sky for days at a time.

9. Write the letter of the storm clouds.

10. Write the letter of the clouds that have frozen drops of water.

11. Which letter shows the place that has the warmest waters?

12. Which letter shows the place that is closest to the equator?

13. Which letter shows the place that is closest to a pole?

14. Is the North Pole or the South Pole closer to that letter?

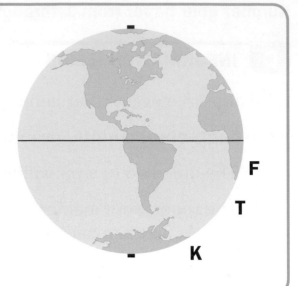

15. The earth makes a circle around the sun one time every ▨ .

16. How many days does it take the earth to make one full circle around the sun?

17. During the winter at the North Pole, how much does the sun shine?

    • never   • all the time

18. During the summer at the North Pole, how much does the sun shine?

    • never   • all the time

19. Name 2 things that can make an ice chunk drift.

A

1	2	3	4
1. displayed	1. thunder	1. move	1. moaned
2. exhibit	2. shallow	2. movement	2. funnel-shaped
3. mysterious	3. blinding	3. foaming	3. stumbled
4. sucked	4. somehow	4. funnel	4. aloud
	5. lightning	5. half-filled	5. tearing

B

Information About Whirlpools

In today's chapter, you will read about a whirlpool. Here is important information about whirlpools:

- Whirlpools are made up of moving water.
- A whirlpool is shaped like a funnel.

Here is a funnel. A funnel is wide on top and narrow on the bottom.

Here is a whirlpool. A whirlpool is also wide on top and narrow on the bottom.

- The water in a whirlpool spins around and around so anything caught in a whirlpool goes around and around as it moves down.

A Giant Whirlpool

Now it was starting to rain. The small lifeboat was sliding up huge waves and then down the other side of the waves. The same movement over and over made Edna feel sick and dizzy.

Suddenly the boat reached the top of a huge wave, and Carla shouted, "I see land." She pointed.

The lifeboat slid down the wave, and Edna could not see anything but water. Then the boat moved up, up, to the top of another wave. Now Edna could see what Carla had pointed to, but it wasn't land. It was a wave, much bigger than the other waves.

"Hang on," Edna shouted. "A giant wave is coming toward us."

For an instant, everything became bright, as lightning shot through the sky; a boom of thunder followed. The huge wave was now very close to the boat. Edna looked up to the top of it and saw a cliff of water with a white, foaming top.

Somehow, the boat moved up the huge wave—up, up, very fast. And now faster. The boat was moving so fast that Edna couldn't see what was happening. There was more lightning—thunder. Edna had to close her eyes.

The boat wasn't just moving up; it was moving around and around. The boat was moving so fast that Edna could hardly tell which direction was up and which direction was down. But she could see that the boat was now at the top of a huge funnel-shaped cone of water. The boat was being sucked into a giant whirlpool.

Edna tried to say something, but her voice wouldn't work. She pointed down to the bottom of the whirlpool. It seemed to be hundreds of meters below the tiny boat. She was dizzy, very dizzy.

The next things happened very fast—so fast that Edna was never sure exactly what happened or why. First, there were large hailstones—hundreds and hundreds of them. For an instant, Edna noticed them floating in the boat, which was quickly filling up with water. So much hail came down that everything seemed to be white and cold. The hail was hitting the girls, but Edna could

hardly feel it. ⭐ Suddenly, there was a great flash and a great spray of water. The flash was blinding; the spray of water was warm.

Later, Edna thought a lot about that flash and the giant splash that followed. Later she also talked to Carla about it. The girls figured out that the lightning must have hit the water right in front of their boat. The lightning must have hit with so much power that it sent the boat flying through the air. After the flash was the giant splash. That must have been the splash that the boat made

when it came down. The boat must have landed far from the whirlpool.

The hail continued to fall for a few minutes after the giant splash. Then it stopped, and a steady rain began to fall. For hours, the rain came down. The wind died down and the waves became smaller and smaller. Finally the rain stopped— without any warning at all, it stopped. The sea was calm again, and Edna was sick. She didn't want to talk and she didn't want to move. She was dizzy. She was lying near the back of the boat, which was half-filled with water now. Edna moaned, "Ooooh." She wasn't sure she knew where she was anymore.

Carla was in the front of the boat, talking to herself. "I don't believe this," she said over and over. "I don't believe this. I want to go home."

Edna looked over the side of the boat. But she didn't see deep blue water that seemed to go down forever. She saw shallow water and sand. The boat was now in water that was only about a meter deep.

Slowly, Edna looked around. "Land," she said in a weak voice. She pointed to a row of palm trees and a beach that was about half a mile away. "Land," she said again as she stood up and stepped over the side of the boat.

"Land," she said and stumbled into the shallow water. She fell down and then got up and started to wade toward the trees. She wanted to be on land—something that would not rock and bounce and make her dizzy. "Land," she said.

Number your paper from 1 through 18.

SKILL ITEMS

Write the word from the box that means the same thing as the underlined part of each sentence.

hooves	tame	modern	tusks
charging	English	ancient	

1. We visited the very, very old city.

2. My pet goat is not wild.

3. The hunters wanted the elephant's large, curved teeth.

4. We visited a very new city.

The rim of the volcano exploded.

5. What word means **made a bang and flew apart?**

6. What word means **a mountain formed from hot flowing rock**?

7. What word means the **top edge** of the volcano?

8. The earth is shaped like a ▊ .

9. The ▊s are the coldest places on the earth and the ▊ is the hottest place on the earth.

10. At which letter would the winters be very, very cold?

11. At which letter would the winters be very, very hot?

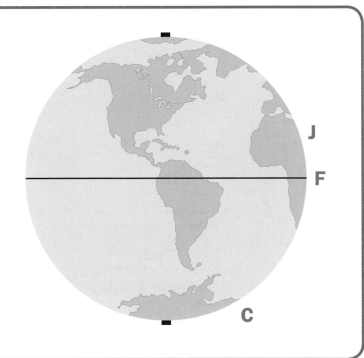

12. Write the letter of the earth that has the North Pole tilting away from the sun.

13. Write the letter of the earth that has the North Pole tilting toward the sun.

14. Write the letter of the earth that has darkness all around the North Pole.

15. Write the letter of the earth that has daylight all around the North Pole.

16. Write **A, B, C,** and **D.** Then write the season each earth in the picture shows.

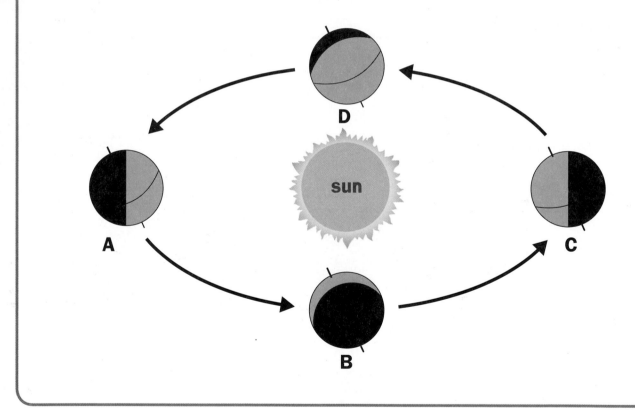

17. Are killer whales fish?

18. Tell if killer whales are **warm-blooded** or **cold-blooded.**

END OF LESSON 27

A

1
1. upright
2. overturned
3. anyone
4. aloud

2
1. tangle
2. gallons
3. ignore
4. strangest
5. bending
6. crowded

3
1. faint
2. hind
3. tearing
4. practice
5. terrible

4
1. exhibit
2. driven
3. mysterious
4. groove
5. displayed

5
1. heavy
2. heaviest
3. light
4. lightest

A Long Night

Carla was pulling the lifeboat toward shore. She called to Edna, "Help me get this boat on shore." Edna stopped and waited for Carla. Then the girls pulled the lifeboat onto the beach and turned it over. Many gallons of salt water spilled out and ran back to the ocean.

The sky was starting to clear. In the distance were heavy clouds, but the waves on the ocean were small. Behind Edna and Carla was a heavy jungle with a great tangle of trees and vines that crowded down to the beach. From the jungle came the sounds of birds and other animals. The whole beach was covered with red sand; Edna had never seen sand like that before.

Edna walked a few feet from the overturned lifeboat and sat down on the soft, red sand beach. "I'm sick," she said.

"I'm sick, too," Carla said as she sat down on the beach.

A few minutes later, Carla was lying down sleeping. Edna had her eyes closed and the world seemed to be spinning around and around. The beach seemed to be rocking. "Oh," she said aloud while she kept her eyes closed and tried to ignore the terrible rocking and spinning.

• • •

"BRRRRAAAAHHHH!"

Edna sat up, her eyes wide. She noticed that it was night, but at first she didn't know where she was.

"BRRRAAAHHH!"

"What's making that noise?" Carla asked.

Edna turned toward Carla's voice, but it was so dark that Edna could hardly see her.

Suddenly, as Edna looked in Carla's direction, she saw something moving out of the jungle. She heard it, too, as it crashed through the vines and trees. There were breaking sounds and tearing sounds as small trees snapped and broke. Edna could see the faint outline of the trees being bent over and snapped down. Suddenly she saw the faint outline of something else, something very large—an animal of some sort. "It can't be," Edna said aloud because the animal that appeared was as big as some of the trees. ★

Edna didn't have much time to look at the animal because it appeared on the beach for only a few seconds. All Edna saw was a very faint outline, but she saw enough to know that she was looking at an animal like nothing she had ever seen before. It was big with a huge head and it seemed to walk upright, on its hind legs.

During the few seconds that Edna saw the animal, it seemed to throw its head back when it roared. Then it suddenly turned around and disappeared into the jungle making a trail of great crashing and bending sounds.

"What was that?" Carla asked.

"I don't know, but I'm scared," Edna answered.

"Yeah," Carla said. "I think we should go hide under the lifeboat."

"Good idea," Edna said.

So the girls crawled under the lifeboat and tried to sleep, but neither girl slept. One time, Edna was almost asleep when Carla moved her foot and made a noise. Edna sat up so suddenly that she hit her head on the inside of the lifeboat.

That was the longest night that Edna remembered, waiting for the sky to become light. She wasn't sure which part of the sky would become light first, because she didn't know where east was. The first part to get light was over the jungle, but it seemed that hours passed before it was light enough to see the ocean clearly. The sun was not up yet, but the birds were squawking and screaming in the jungle.

At last, Edna and Carla crawled out from under the lifeboat. The first thing they did was walk to where they had seen the outline of the huge animal. As soon as they got close to the spot, they saw the animal's huge footprints in the red sand.

When Edna looked at the footprints, she knew that there was an animal on this island that looked like no other living animal anyone had ever seen. It left footprints that were a yard long!

Number your paper from 1 through 22.

C SKILL ITEMS

Write the word from the box that means the same thing as the underlined part of each sentence.

speech	excited	screech	box
certain	armor	pouch	surface

1. She put her keys in the <u>small bag</u>.

2. The <u>sharp sound</u> of the peacock startled me.

3. I am <u>sure</u> about the answer to the question.

Use the words in the box to write complete sentences you've learned.

volcano	practiced	attracted	exploded
	sense	immediately	loudly

4. The smell ▓▓▓ flies ▓▓▓ .

5. The rim of the ▓▓▓ ▓▓▓ .

D REVIEW ITEMS

6. What season is it at the North Pole when the North Pole tilts toward the sun?

7. What season is it at the North Pole when the North Pole tilts away from the sun?

8. Female animals fight in the spring to protect ▓▓▓ .

9. Name 2 kinds of Alaskan animals that are dangerous in the spring.

10. Name 3 animals that are warm-blooded.

11. Name 3 animals that are cold-blooded.

12. What are clouds made of?

13. What kind of cloud does the picture show?

14. What happens to a drop of water at **B?**

15. Which object went into the pile **first?**

16. Which object went into the pile **last?**

17. Which object went into the pile **earlier,** the cup or the book?

18. Which object went into the pile **earlier,** the bone or the book?

19. Which object went into the pile **just after** the pencil?

20. Which object went into the pile **just after** the bone?

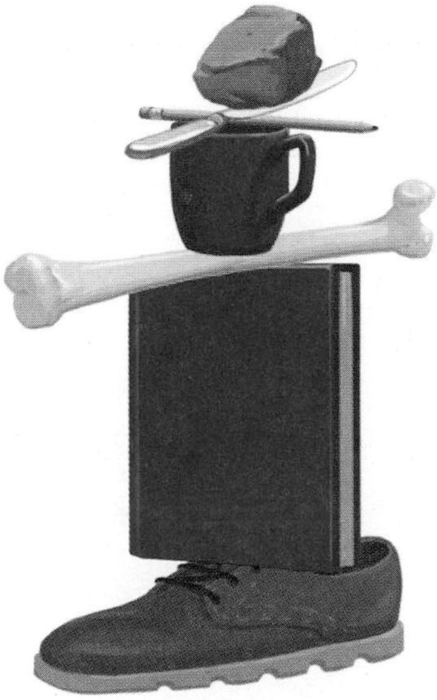

21. Whirlpools are made up of moving ______.

22. A whirlpool is shaped like a ______.

END OF LESSON 28

A

1
1. breath
2. shriek
3. leathery
4. immediately

2
1. clearing
2. dents
3. driven
4. practiced
5. terrible
6. terribly

3
1. sense
2. pond
3. club
4. thick
5. spread
6. stared

4
1. groove
2. grove
3. steam
4. stream
5. tail
6. trail

Footprints

There were footprints of a huge animal in the red sand—footprints that were a yard long. Each footprint had three toes. The size of the footprints told Edna something about the size of the animal. The footprints also made very deep dents in the sand. These deep dents told Edna something about how much the animal weighed.

Between the footprints was a deep groove in the sand. Carla asked, "What could make that deep trail in the sand?"

Suddenly Edna shouted, "A tail— I'll bet a tail did that. That animal is walking on its hind legs and it's dragging a heavy tail behind it. The tail makes that deep groove in the sand."

For a while, the girls walked around the footprints and didn't say anything. Then they looked toward the jungle and saw that the animal had left a huge path through the jungle. On either side of this path were thick vines and trees, but the path was almost clear. It looked as if somebody had driven a truck through the jungle and knocked down all the small trees and vines.

✿ Edna said, "I don't think we should go into that jungle."

"Yeah, we shouldn't do it," Carla said. The girls were silent for a few moments as they stood there and looked at the great path that led into the jungle. Then Carla said, "But we could follow that path for a little way. We don't have to go too far."

"I don't want to go in there," Edna said. But she wasn't telling Carla the truth. Although part of her was frightened and wanted to run away, part of her wanted to see what made those huge footprints. Her mind made pictures of that animal. In one of the pictures, the animal was chasing ✿ Carla and Edna, who were running as fast as they could, but the animal was getting closer and closer and . . .

"Come on," Carla said. "Let's go just a little way."

Now another part of Edna's mind was taking over; this part wanted to see the animal and was not terribly frightened. It made up pictures of Carla and Edna sneaking up on the animal. In these pictures, the animal did not see Edna and Carla. ✦ "This animal is not very smart," Edna said to herself. "If it was a smart animal, it would have found us last night. Maybe it does not have a good sense of smell or maybe it has poor eyes."

"Okay, let's follow the path," Edna said to Carla. "But just a little way."

Carla picked up a short, heavy branch and practiced swinging it like a club. Edna picked up a branch too. They were easy to find in the path made by the animal.

So the girls started down the path into the jungle, walking very slowly and carefully. They jumped each time a screech or a roar came from the jungle. They tried not to step on small branches that would make a cracking sound. Slowly, they moved farther into the jungle. Soon, Edna could not see the beach behind her because the trees above the girls blocked out the light.

"This is far enough," Edna said after she realized they had gone over a hundred meters into the jungle.

"Shhh," Carla said, and pointed straight ahead. Edna could see a clearing with a small pond in the middle of it. From the pond, steam rose into the air. As the girls moved forward, Edna could see a small stream flowing into the pond. And she saw tall grass.

When the girls reached the edge of the clearing, Edna stopped because she noticed that the trees were very strange. She looked at a small tree on the edge of the clearing. "I saw a picture of a tree like this somewhere," she said to herself, "but I can't remember where." She tried to remember. Suddenly, she remembered the tree and where it was. And when she remembered, she wanted to run from the jungle as fast as she could. She had seen a picture of that tree in a book on dinosaurs. She had looked at the picture in the book many times, and she clearly remembered the tree. It was in a picture that showed Tyrannosaurus fighting with Triceratops.

Edna looked at the tree and suddenly realized what had made the huge footprints. "Oh no," she said aloud.

Number your paper from 1 through 23.

C REVIEW ITEMS

1. When days get longer, is the North Pole tilting toward the sun or away from the sun?

2. When days get shorter, is the North Pole tilting toward the sun or away from the sun?

3. In April, the sun shines for more than ▮▮▮ hours each day in Alaska.

---

4. Which globe shows how the earth looks on the first day of winter?

5. Which globe shows how the earth looks on the first day of summer?

R

sun

K

Use these names to answer the questions:

Tyrannosaurus, Triceratops.

6. What is animal X?

7. What is animal Y?

X

Y

---

8. Which came **earlier** on the earth, dinosaurs or horses?

9. Which came **earlier** on the earth, strange sea animals or dinosaurs?

10. Write the letter of the layer that went into the pile **first.**

11. Write the letter of the layer that went into the pile **next.**

12. Write the letter of the layer that went into the pile **last.**

13. Which layer went into the pile **earlier,** B or C?

14. Which layer went into the pile **earlier,** A or C?

15. Write the letter of the layer where we would find the skeletons of humans.

16. Write the letter of the layer that has dinosaur skeletons.

17. Write the letter of the layer where we would find the skeletons of horses.

18. Write the letter of the layer we live on.

19. What's the name of layer C?

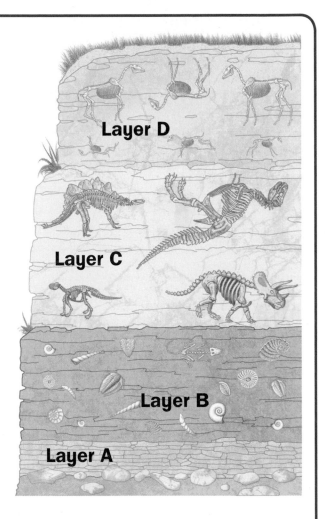

20. What kind of animals lived in the Mesozoic?

21. Captain Parker's ship passed through a place where hundreds of ships have sunk or been lost. Name that place.

22. Write the letters of the 3 things you find in the Bermuda Triangle.

  a. streams

  b. ice floes

  c. huge waves

  d. sudden storms

  e. mountains

  f. whirlpools

23. What happens to something that gets caught in a whirlpool?

END OF LESSON 29

A

1

1. deafening
2. admit
3. emperor
4. carriage
5. fabric

2

1. magnificent
2. splendid
3. flattering
4. tailor
5. empress

3

1. busiest
2. differently
3. wisest
4. exciting
5. actually

4

1. puzzled
2. reminded
3. swelled
4. hearted
5. naked
6. neared

5

1. wherever
2. clever
3. route
4. indeed
5. clothing
6. parade

6

1. embarrass
2. embarrassment
3. invisible
4. jacket
5. instant
6. jealous

The Emperor's New Clothes

Retold by Lucas Novak
Illustrated by Szilvia Szakall

Once there lived a very rich and powerful emperor. The emperor was a kind and good-hearted ruler, but he had a strange interest. He loved clothes, and he had more clothes than anyone in the land. He had so many clothes that they filled most of the closets and rooms in his palace. The emperor had three tailors who spent all their time making new clothes for him.

The emperor spent his time differently. He loved to look at himself in his fine clothing. The halls of the palace were lined with mirrors, and every room had several large mirrors so the emperor could see himself wherever he went in the palace.

One day a clever thief came to the palace. The
thief was dressed like a tailor. He told the guards that
he had the finest fabric the emperor had ever seen.

A guard led the thief to the emperor. The thief quickly told the emperor, "You must not let your other tailors know about the fabric I have to show you. If they know, they will become very jealous and will make up lies to try to change the way you think about the suit I can make for you."

The emperor said, "The other tailors will not know about the fabric or the suit."

The thief said, "The fabric I will show you is not only wonderful—it is magic. Only the wisest people in the land can see this fabric. Fools will not see it. To them, the fabric will look invisible."

The thief opened his bag and pretended to hold up some fabric. "There," the thief said. "Isn't that magnificent?"

Of course, the emperor could see nothing. But he did not admit that he saw nothing, because he did not want to look like a fool. So he pretended to see a wonderful fabric. "Oh, oh, isn't that exciting," he said. "Yes, it is wonderful."

The thief pretended to make a fine suit of clothes with pants, a jacket, and a robe. Then the thief pretended to hand the clothes to the emperor, and the emperor pretended to put them on. The emperor paid the thief 20 gold coins for the new suit. This was more than he had ever paid for a suit, but the thief reminded him that nobody had ever seen such a suit before.

The empress was shocked when she saw the emperor standing naked in front of the mirror. He said, "My dear, I know that you can see my wonderful new clothes because you are no fool. Fools cannot see this magic fabric, but I'm sure that you can."

"Oh, indeed I can," she said. "It's very unusual, isn't it?"

The emperor was afraid to take off his magic suit that night because he was afraid that he would not be able to see it or even feel it again.

The next day, the emperor ordered a great parade so he could show everybody in the land his wonderful new clothes.

People came from all over. Most of them had already heard that fools were not able to see the magic fabric, so when they saw the naked emperor passing by in his splendid carriage, they made flattering comments. "My, my, what a handsome suit," they said. "It's like nothing I've ever seen before." But the people who lined the streets did not cheer the way they would cheer if they saw something wonderful. After they pretended to see something wonderful, they quickly became quiet, staring at the emperor with puzzled eyes.

If the crowd had not been so quiet, people probably would not have heard what the little child said. As the emperor neared the busiest street on the parade route, a little child looked up at the emperor and asked, "Mother, why doesn't the emperor have any clothes on?"

The people in the crowd heard the child. So did the emperor. In an instant, he knew the child was right. The emperor realized that he was naked. In the same instant, all the people in the crowd realized that they had been fools for not saying what they actually saw. At first only a few of them laughed, but the laughter swelled, and soon the sound of people laughing was deafening. The emperor nearly died of embarrassment. He darted from the carriage and ran all the way back to his palace, but he could still hear the laughter.

For three weeks after that day, he did not leave the palace or see anyone. When he finally came out of hiding, he had changed. He didn't care as much about clothes, and he was a wiser ruler. From that bitter parade, he had learned a valuable lesson: pretending does not change the way things really are.

A

1

1. <u>half</u>-folded
2. <u>ea</u>gle
3. <u>for</u>got
4. <u>mon</u>ster
5. <u>mouth</u>ful
6. <u>foot</u>print

2

1. arrangement
2. automatically
3. leathery
4. breaths
5. instantly
6. immediately

3

1. started
2. stared
3. sailed
4. slid
5. spread
6. attract
7. lying

The Monster

Just as Edna was going to tell Carla about the tree and the dinosaurs in the book, a loud flapping sound came from the sky. A huge bird-like animal sailed down from above the jungle. Edna knew it wasn't a bird because it didn't have feathers; it had large wings that looked like leather. The animal also had large sharp teeth. As the flying animal got close to the ground, Edna could see that it was very big—bigger than an eagle. The flying animal flapped its leathery wings loudly as it landed in the middle of the clearing where the girls could see it more clearly.

Carla whispered, "What is that thing?"

Edna said, "It's an animal that lived a hundred million years ago."

Edna and Carla stared at the animal, which was on a rock with its wings half-folded and its mouth open.

"Let's get out of here," Edna whispered.

The girls began to sneak down the path toward the beach when suddenly, the ground shook and there was a terrible crashing sound. Edna couldn't tell where the sound was coming from so she ran from the path and hid behind a vine-covered tree. Then she realized that the crashing sound was moving closer and closer; it was coming from the beach and moving along the path toward the clearing. A small tree crashed to the ground right in front of Edna. Above her she could see the form of a monster standing in the path that Edna and Carla had followed. Edna could smell the animal which smelled something like garbage. Edna instantly recognized the animal—Tyrannosaurus.

The monster moved so quickly that Edna could hardly believe it. Like lightning, it turned its head one way and then another. Its mouth was open and it seemed to be smiling with teeth as big as knives. The huge, bird-like animal in the clearing also saw the monster and spread its wings and started to flap them. Immediately Tyrannosaurus turned its head in the direction of the winged animal and an instant later, was running toward it.

With each step, the ground shook. As Tyrannosaurus ran, its huge tail followed and hit the tree that Edna was standing behind. The tree cracked and Edna went flying into the soft plants that covered the floor of the jungle. Before Edna could stand up, she heard noises from the clearing—a leathery flapping sound, then a terrible crunching sound, like the sound of bones being crushed. There were three squawking sounds and then more crunching sounds.

Edna got up and started to run down the path toward the beach. She made her legs move as fast as they could and she kept telling them to move faster. She told herself, "Get out of here. Get out of here." She tripped and almost fell. "Don't fall," she told herself. "Run," she told herself and she continued running as fast as she could.

She wasn't thinking about the noise she made as she ran; she wasn't thinking that Tyrannosaurus might hear her; she wasn't thinking about anything but running. "Run," she told herself, "and don't slow down."

She noticed that there was a large yellow-and-black snake on the path right in front of her. It was at least three meters long, but she didn't even slow down. With a great leap she jumped over the snake and kept on running. When the girls had gone into the jungle, the path had seemed long. Now it seemed even longer, as if it would never end. "Run," she said out loud between her breaths.

Edna ran until she could see the beach ahead of her. Then her mind slowly began to work again. She stopped and turned around. She looked as hard as she could, but she saw nothing on the path behind her. Tyrannosaurus was making so much noise eating that flying animal that it couldn't hear Edna. Besides, Tyrannosaurus already had a huge meal. What would it want with a tiny animal like Edna? Edna wouldn't be much more than a mouthful for the monster. She walked out onto the red sand of the beach and noticed that she was out of breath. Now she began to realize how frightened she had been. She had been so frightened that she forgot about everything. Suddenly, Edna turned all the way around and realized she had forgotten about Carla. Where was Carla?

Edna looked in all directions, but she couldn't see Carla.

Number your paper from 1 through 20.

C SKILL ITEMS

Here are three events that happened in the story.

Write **beginning, middle,** or **end** for each event.

1. Edna went flying into the soft plants that covered the floor of the jungle.

2. A huge bird-like animal sailed down from above the jungle.

3. She had been so frightened that she forgot about everything.

STORY ITEMS

4. Write the letter of the footprint made by the lightest animal.

5. Write the letter of the footprint made by the heaviest animal.

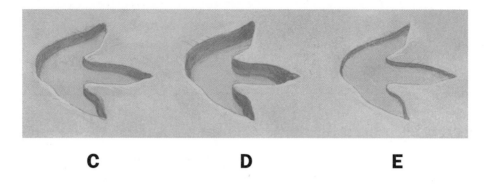

C   D   E

The picture shows marks left by an animal.

6. Which arrow shows the direction the animal is moving?

7. Write the letter of the part that shows a footprint.

8. Write the letter of the part that shows the mark left by the animal's tail.

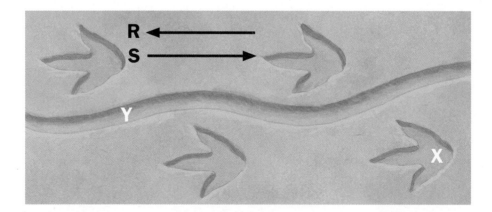

9. About how long are killer whales?

10. Compare the size of killer whales with the size of other whales.

11. Are killer whales fish?

12. Tell if killer whales are **warm-blooded** or **cold-blooded.**

13. Name 2 things that can make an ice chunk drift.

14. In which direction will you drift when you're in an ocean current?

15. In which direction will you drift when you're in a strong wind?

16. What kind of boat do Inuits use in the summer?

17. Why don't they use those boats in the winter?

18. Write the letter of the storm clouds.

19. Write the letter of the clouds that may stay in the sky for days at a time.

20. Write the letter of the clouds that have frozen drops of water.

A   B   C

END OF LESSON 31

A

1
1. cough
2. pour
3. volcano
4. neither
5. adventure
6. supplies

2
1. remains
2. shriek
3. reason
4. attract
5. safety
6. automatically

3
1. lying
2. laying
3. breathe
4. breath
5. pacing
6. packing

4
1. glanced
2. prancing
3. strangely
4. untangle
5. arrangement
6. eastern
7. harden

B Chapter 8

Looking for Carla

Carla was not in sight. That meant that Carla was still back there in the jungle. Edna took a couple of steps into the jungle; then she stopped and looked down the path. She couldn't see anything and part of her mind told her, "Don't go back there—you'll get killed." Then another part of her mind said, "You've got to help Carla—go back."

For a moment Edna thought of calling to Carla, but then she

realized that the sound of her voice would attract the monster.

Suddenly, she noticed that she was walking back toward the clearing. She had decided to try to help her friend, so she crouched over and kept near the side of the path. She was ready to duck behind a tree as soon as she spotted Tyrannosaurus. She couldn't hear anything except her breath and the sounds of her feet moving through the green plants. Step, step, step—she moved down the path.

A beautiful flower caught her eye. The flower was growing in the middle of the path, and she noticed that the birds in the jungle were not squawking. "Why are they silent?" she asked herself.

She answered, "They probably flew away when Tyrannosaurus ran into the clearing."

Then once again she noticed how quiet it was as she walked—step, step, step. Edna was nearly all the way back to the clearing when she heard Tyrannosaurus. She could smell the dinosaur, too, but she couldn't see it.

Edna ducked behind a tree on the side of the path. Now her mind started to imagine some of the things that might have happened.

Maybe Tyrannosaurus had already found Carla and maybe Tyrannosaurus . . . "No," she told

herself, "don't think about things like that. Carla is all right."

Edna stayed behind the tree for a minute or two. During that time, Tyrannosaurus didn't seem to be moving toward her. So, slowly she snuck back onto the path and moved toward the sound of the breathing—closer and closer. Then she saw Carla lying near the path. Her leg was tangled up in some vines and she was lying very still.

Part of Edna's mind said this: "Carla is not moving, so she is dead."

Another part of Edna's mind said this: "No, she is not dead, and she is not hurt. She is lying very still because Tyrannosaurus is very near and she doesn't want to move." Edna snuck up a little closer and now she could see Tyrannosaurus. The dinosaur was at the edge of the clearing, looking in the direction of Carla. But the dinosaur was not standing still; it was pacing and turning its head from one side to another, as if it was looking for something.

Edna looked at Carla and knew that she was all right. She was lying still because she knew that Tyrannosaurus was searching for her.

On the far end of the clearing were the remains of the flying dinosaur. For some reason, Tyrannosaurus was not eating them.

Suddenly, Edna got an idea of how to save Carla. The plan was very dangerous, but Edna felt strangely brave. She felt that she had to try to help Carla. Edna's plan was to attract the dinosaur's attention by going into the jungle and making loud noises. Tyrannosaurus would be attracted by the noise and would come after it. When the dinosaur followed the noise, Carla would be able to untangle herself and run to safety.

Edna's heart was pounding because she knew that she would have to move very fast. She remembered how fast Tyrannosaurus moved through the jungle.

Suddenly, Tyrannosaurus turned around and looked at three Triceratops dinosaurs that came into the clearing. They held their heads down as they moved toward Tyrannosaurus. Tyrannosaurus ran toward them and then stopped, opened its mouth very wide, and let out a terrible shriek.

"Move," Edna told herself as she ran toward Carla, who was already sitting up and trying to untangle her leg.

Edna grabbed the vines and tried to pull them free, but it seemed to take forever. Carla didn't say anything as the girls tugged at the vines and tried to get Carla's leg free. The dinosaurs were very close to them.

Number your paper from 1 through 22.

Write the word from the box that means the same thing as the underlined part of each sentence.

armor	gulped	shabby	docked
graph	mast	bailed	boots

1. He <u>quickly swallowed</u> the milk.

2. She got some new <u>mukluks</u>.

3. The animal's <u>hard covering</u> protects it from other animals.

The new exhibit displayed mysterious fish.

4. What word describes **things we don't understand?**

5. What word means **an arrangement of things for people to look at?**

6. What word means **showed?**

7. How long ago did dinosaurs live on the earth?

   • 30 thousand years ago

   • 1 million years ago

   • 100 million years ago

8. In what season are animals most dangerous in Alaska?

9. During what season do female animals in Alaska have babies?

10. About how long are killer whales?

11. Compare the size of killer whales with the size of other whales.

Write the name of each animal in the picture.

12.

13.

15.

14.

16.

17.

18. Which animal in the picture is the biggest?

19. Which animal is the smallest?

20. The map shows a route. What state is at the north end of the route?

21. What country is at the south end of the route?

22. About how many miles is the route?

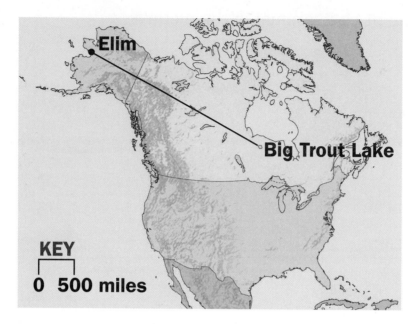

KEY

0   500 miles

A

1	2	3	4
1. <u>how</u>ever	1. hardened	1. relax	1. backing
2. <u>ex</u>plodes	2. glanced	2. experience	2. rowed
3. <u>under</u>water	3. billowed	3. quake	3. exploding
4. <u>vol</u>cano	4. divided	4. swift	4. softer
5. <u>cough</u>ing	5. directed	5. explosion	5. pressing
6. <u>eas</u>tern		6. pours	6. prancing
		7. thud	

B

Information About Volcanos and Earthquakes

You will be reading about volcanos and earthquakes. A volcano is a mountain that was made of hot melted rock. That rock comes from inside the earth.

The picture shows what a volcano would look like if it were cut in half and we could see the inside.

There is a layer of melted rock in the earth far below the volcano. The melted rock moves up to the surface of the earth. When the melted rock pours out onto the surface of the earth, the rock cools and becomes hard. More melted rock piles up on top of the hardened rock. The volcano keeps growing in the shape of a cone.

The volcano may pour out great clouds of smoke.

Sometimes a volcano explodes. Sometimes there are earthquakes around volcanos.

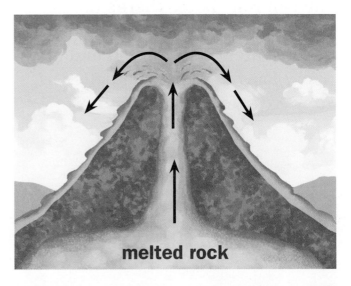

melted rock

Explosion

Carla and Edna were tugging at the vines that were tangled around Carla's leg. The vines were like thick, sticky ropes that wouldn't let go. Occasionally, Edna glanced up and looked at what was happening in the clearing. The three Triceratops dinosaurs were lined up, waiting for Tyrannosaurus to attack them. The giant Tyrannosaurus was prancing around with its mouth wide open moving toward the Triceratops dinosaurs and then backing away. From time to time, it would let out a terrible shriek.

Just after Tyrannosaurus's third shriek, Carla's leg was free. "Take her hand and help her up," Edna said to herself. "Now run but keep an eye on her. Let her run in front of you. She's not running fast enough, so push her on the back to help her run faster. Is that as fast as she can run? Look, there's the beach. Run right down to the edge of the water. Turn around and look back. They're not coming after us, so we're safe."

The girls stood near the edge of the water for a few minutes, listening to the sounds that came from the jungle. The sounds told them that a terrible fight was going on. Tyrannosaurus would shriek from time to time. Suddenly there was a great thud and the shriek of Tyrannosaurus turned into a cry. Just then the whole island seemed to shake.

The tops of the trees began to shake so hard that coconuts fell to the ground. Suddenly, hundreds of birds left the island, flying to the west. A few moments later the ground shook with such force that Edna fell down. The red beach moved up and then down, then it rocked to one side and then to the other.

"It's an earthquake!" Carla yelled as some trees near the edge of the jungle fell over.

Edna sat up and noticed a great cloud of smoke over the top of the island. She pointed to the smoke and shouted, "Volcano!"

The smoke boiled and billowed into the air with great speed. Within a few seconds, it had covered the whole eastern part of the sky, and still the smoke cloud was growing.

"Come on," Edna shouted as she ran toward the boat. The beach suddenly shook. She stumbled, fell, and slid through the red sand. She got up and ran. The sky was now becoming dark, as the enormous cloud continued to grow.

The girls reached the boat and turned it over as fast as they could and pushed it into the shallow water. When they were a few meters from the shore, a terrible quake shook the island. It made a large crack in the sandy beach, which moved out into the water, right under the boat. Suddenly, Edna noticed that the sand under her feet had disappeared. She slipped underwater and felt her feet being pulled into a swift current.

Edna reached up and tried to grab something. Her hand grabbed a rope that was attached to the front of the boat and she held on to the rope with all her might. The currents were spinning her around, but she kept a tight grip on the rope. Slowly she pulled herself up to the boat. She was coughing and trying to catch her breath.

Between coughs, she called, "Carla, Carla!" She had salt water in her eyes, so she couldn't see well.

"I'm here," Carla answered, but she couldn't see where she was.

Edna rubbed her eyes with one hand and looked in the direction of the voice. Carla was sitting in the boat. She helped Edna get into the boat. The sky was so dark now that it was almost like night.

Suddenly, there was a terrible explosion that had so much force it seemed to press the air against Edna's face. This pressing feeling came before the sound of the explosion. The sound was like nothing that Edna had ever heard. The sound was so loud that her ears would ring for hours. That explosion had so much force that it knocked down all the trees on the island.

As the girls rowed away from the island, Carla asked, "Where are we going to go?"

"I don't know," Edna replied. "I don't know." She did know one thing, however; she knew that she didn't want to be near that exploding island.

Number your paper from 1 through 25.

D SKILL ITEMS

Use the words in the box to write complete sentences.

displayed	adventure	exploded	reason
rim	glanced	mysterious	directed

1. The _____ of the volcano _____ .
2. The new exhibit _____ _____ fish.

E REVIEW ITEMS

3. What season is it at the North Pole when the North Pole tilts toward the sun?
4. What season is it at the North Pole when the North Pole tilts away from the sun?
5. In what season are animals most dangerous in Alaska?
6. During what season do female animals in Alaska have babies?
7. Things closer to the bottom of the pile went into the pile _____ .

8. Write the letter of the layer that went into the pile first.

9. Write the letter of the layer that we live on.

10. Which layer went into the pile later, **A** or **B**?

11. Write the letter of the layer where we would find the skeletons of humans.

12. Write the letter of the layer where we find the skeletons of dinosaurs.

13. Write the letter of the layer where we find the skeletons of horses.

14. What's the name of layer **C**?

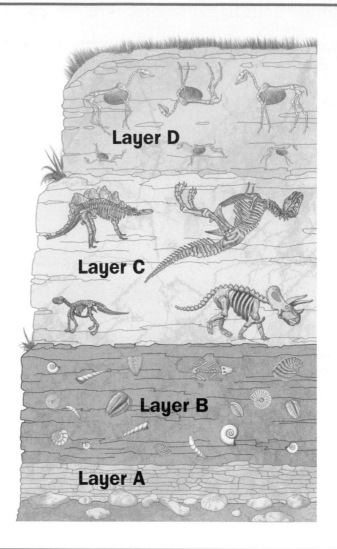

Use the names to answer the questions:

Tyrannosaurus, Triceratops.

15. What is animal **R**?

16. What is animal **S**?

17. What are clouds made of?

18. What kind of cloud does the picture show?

19. What happens to a drop of water at **B?**

20. The picture shows half a hailstone. How many times did the stone go through a cloud?

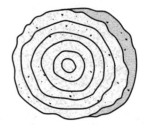

21. Which letter on the map shows Alaska?

22. Which letter shows Canada?

23. Which letter shows the main part of the United States?

24. Which 2 letters show where Inuits live?

25. How warm is it during winter in Alaska?

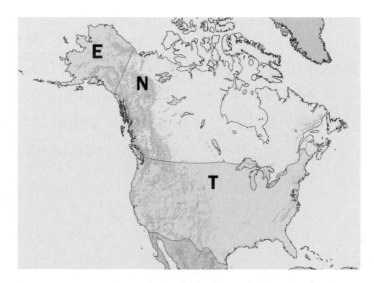

END OF LESSON 33

A

1	2	3	4
1. approach	1. <u>bli</u>sters	1. throat	1. experience
2. bandage	2. <u>adventure</u>	2. chew	2. billowing
3. laundry	3. <u>un</u>real	3. nor	3. neither
4. stomach	4. <u>deep</u>est	4. rim	4. fade
5. mysterious	5. <u>shad</u>ow	5. beneath	5. relax
6. Tuesday	6. <u>sup</u>plies	6. honestly	

B

Underlined Words

Some of the words in stories you will read must be spoken loudly. Here's the rule about words that must be spoken louder than other words: **The words that must be spoken louder are underlined.**

The following sentences have underlined words. Remember to say the underlined words in a loud voice; say the other words in a soft voice.

a. That is <u>wrong</u>.

b. You are a <u>crook</u>.

c. I am <u>not</u> a crook.

d. I'm <u>tired</u> of reading.

e. My name is <u>Sam</u>.

f. <u>My</u> name is Sam, <u>too</u>.

g. This book is <u>hard</u>.

h. If you think <u>your</u> book is hard, try reading <u>this</u> book.

i. You sure like to <u>talk</u>.

Back in the Lifeboat

The lifeboat was floating on a bright, shining sea that was so calm that it looked almost as if it was made of glass. When Edna looked down, she could see different colors. Where the water was not very deep, the color was bright green. Deeper spots were blue, with the deepest spots dark blue or purple. The sun pounded down on the girls. Edna had blisters on her hands from rowing, but she was not rowing now, just sitting and trying to relax. In the far distance, a billowing cloud rose high into the sky. Edna searched for the island but could no longer see it.

As she sat there in the lifeboat, she realized that they didn't have supplies. There were no other islands in sight and the boat seemed to be drifting in a current that was taking it to the west. But how long would it be before the girls spotted another island, and what would they do if they didn't find land soon? Edna was already starting to feel thirsty. She tried not to think about it, but when she swallowed, she noticed that her throat was dry.

Neither Edna nor Carla had said anything for a long time. The adventure they had on the island was so unreal that Edna didn't know exactly what to say.

Suddenly, Edna noticed that the boat was drifting faster, and when she looked to the west, she got a very sick feeling. In the distance, she could see the rim of a whirlpool. She also noticed that the boat was moving toward it, speeding faster and faster, through the green water.

The rushing sounds from the whirlpool got louder and louder. Now the boat was moving over the rim of the whirlpool. "Hang on," Edna shouted, as she grabbed on to the side of the boat and hung on with all her might. The boat sped around and around in the whirlpool. When Edna looked up at the sky, the clouds seemed to be spinning around and around. ★ The boat was going deeper and deeper into the whirlpool.

Suddenly Edna noticed a great cone of water above the boat. The boat was spinning so fast that its force pressed Edna against the bottom of the boat. She felt so sick and dizzy that she squeezed her eyes closed as tightly as she could. Then the sounds seemed to fade away and everything went dark.

•   •   •

The first thing Edna noticed was heat, terrible heat. "Where am I?" she

said aloud. Then she realized that she was lying in the bottom of the lifeboat and the sun was beating down on her face. The boat was not moving and the water around the boat was still. As she sat up, she realized that there was some water in the bottom of the boat. The water was very warm.

Edna looked over at Carla and asked, "Are you okay?"

Carla looked very sick as she said, "I think so, but what happened?"

"I don't know," Edna answered. "We were in a whirlpool, and that's the last thing I remember. Do you think we are dead?"

"No, I don't think we're dead," Carla replied. "But I don't remember how we got out of the whirlpool. I must have passed out."

 "I passed out, too," Edna answered. Slowly, she turned around and looked at the calm ocean. She didn't see any signs of whirlpools or billowing clouds. "We must be far from the island," Edna said.

Edna looked over the side of the boat, into the dark blue water. She could see some fish swimming around beneath the boat. They seemed to like swimming in the shadow of the boat. As Edna looked at the fish, she remembered something she had once read. Fish have a lot of fresh water in them. If you chew on raw fish, you can squeeze the water out. Edna didn't like the idea of chewing on raw fish, but she ✿ knew that without water, she and Carla would not last for more than a few more hours in the hot sun.

Number your paper from 1 through 23.

D **SKILL ITEMS**

Write the word or words from the box that mean the same thing as the underlined part of each sentence.

| shriek | breath | swift | armor |
| skeletons | an instant | a sense | tangle |

1. The animal <u>bones</u> were near the big old tree.

2. He was afraid for <u>a moment</u>.

3. The runner was <u>very fast</u>.

4. Write the letters of the 3 things you find in the Bermuda Triangle.

   a. sudden storms   d. mountains

   b. whirlpools   e. streams

   c. ice floes   f. huge waves

---

5. Write the letter of the footprint made by the heaviest animal.

6. Write the letter of the footprint made by the lightest animal.

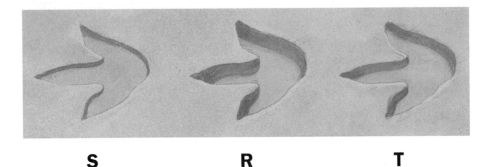

       S   **R**   **T**

---

7. How long ago did dinosaurs live on the earth?

   • 10 million years ago

   • 100 million years ago

   • 100 thousand years ago

8. Two things happen to melted rock when it moves down the sides of a volcano. Name those 2 things.

9. What is it called when the earth shakes and cracks?

10. The earth makes a circle around the sun one time every ▭ .

11. How many days does it take the earth to make one full circle around the sun?

12. Is it easier to fly alone or with a large flock?

13. Flying near the back of a large flock is like riding your bike ▭ .

    • with the wind   • against the wind

14. During winter at the North Pole, how much does the sun shine?

    • never   • all the time

15. During summer at the North Pole, how much does the sun shine?

    • never   • all the time

Write the name of each animal in the picture.

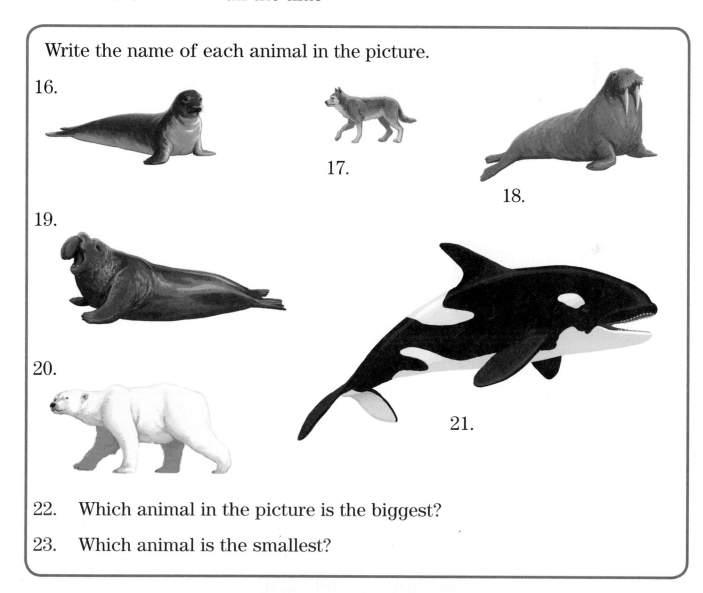

16.

17.

18.

19.

20.

21.

22. Which animal in the picture is the biggest?

23. Which animal is the smallest?

A

1
1. actually
2. exhibit
3. museum
4. Leonard
5. character
6. embarrassed

2
1. underwater
2. overboard
3. somehow
4. automobile

3
1. experiences
2. divided
3. hugging
4. approached
5. honestly

4
1. directed
2. bandages
3. paying
4. sandwiches
5. handful

5
1. Monday
2. laundry
3. yesterday
4. mysterious
5. stomach
6. Tuesday
7. possible

B Chapter 11

Saved

Edna realized that she and Carla needed water because they would not last for more than a few hours without it. Edna crawled to the front of the boat and started to look for fishing gear, but then she noticed a slim line of smoke in the distance. It wasn't the billowing smoke that had come from the island. "A ship," Edna shouted as she stood up and pointed. "I think there's a ship over there."

Carla stood up and looked in the direction Edna pointed. "You're right, I can see it, and I think it's coming toward us."

The next hour seemed longer than any hour Edna ever remembered. The only thing she and Carla did during that hour was watch the approaching ship. Edna believed that if she stopped watching, the ship would disappear. As it got closer, she recognized the ship. "That's Dad's ship," she shouted, "they're coming back for us."

• • •

The crew members helped Edna and Carla climb from the lifeboat onto the deck of the ship. Captain Parker put his arms around the girls, and Edna started to cry. She didn't want to cry and she hadn't cried once during the whole adventure. But now that she was safe and her dad was hugging her, she couldn't help it. "Dad," she said in a soft voice as tears ran down her cheeks. She was so glad to be back, and she was ashamed for not paying attention to what her father had warned them about.

"I'm glad we found you," Captain Parker said. "Now let's get you taken care of."

Both girls had blisters on their hands from rowing and both were badly sunburned. They were also very hungry and thirsty, but within an hour, they were fixed up—with burn cream on their noses, little bandages on their hands, food and water in their stomachs. Now Edna was finishing her third glass of juice. Carla had eaten two sandwiches, and she almost finished a huge piece of pie. But she couldn't make it through that pie. She pushed herself away from the table and stood up. "I'm full," she said.

"I'd like to talk with you girls," Captain Parker said. The girls followed him to the map room where he told them to sit down. "All right," he said, "can you explain exactly what happened?"

"I know we shouldn't have been playing around with the lifeboat," Carla said. ★ "But I'm the one to blame because Edna didn't want to do it."

"Just tell me what happened," Captain Parker said. So the girls told the whole story: how the boat fell into the water, how they got sucked into the whirlpool, how they found the mysterious island, and what happened on the island.

After the girls had finished telling about the second whirlpool, Carla said, "I don't know how we got out of the whirlpool, but we did, somehow. Then the next thing we knew, your ship was coming back toward us."

"That's some story," Captain Parker said. "Do you honestly think all those things happened?"

"Oh yeah," Edna said, "we're not making it up; it really happened, the whole thing."

Then Carla asked, "Don't you believe us?"

Captain Parker smiled. "From the way you tell the story, I think you believe it. But I'm not sure it actually happened that way because some of your experiences are impossible."

"It did happen, Dad," Edna said, "it really did. Everything we told you is true."

"Well then, tell me this," Captain Parker said. "What day of the week was it when you went overboard?"

"Monday," Edna replied.

"And is it correct that you spent a night on the island?"

"Yes," Edna agreed.

Captain Parker said, "So what day would that make today?"

"Today is Tuesday," Edna said.

Captain Parker opened a door and shouted to a crew member, "Tell these girls what day today is."

The man looked a little puzzled as he answered, "Monday."

"Monday?" Edna said. "No, that was yesterday. Today is Tuesday."

The young crew member smiled and said, "What is this, some kind of joke?"

Captain Parker said, "No, everything is all right. Thank you."

Carla said to Edna, "It can't be Monday."

"But it is Monday," Captain Parker said. "You may have had too much sun out there because it has only been five hours since you left the ship."

"But it really happened, Dad," Edna said.

Later that afternoon, Edna was taking her wet clothes to the laundry room. As she approached the laundry room, she checked the pockets of her pants. She turned one pocket inside out and suddenly she stopped. About a handful of wet red sand fell onto the deck of the ship. If the adventure hadn't happened, how did that sand get into her pocket?

Edna never found the answer to that question.

THE END

Number your paper from 1 through 22.

C SKILL ITEMS

Here are three events that happened in this chapter.

Write **beginning, middle,** or **end** for each event.

1. In the distance was a slim line of smoke.

2. Captain Parker opened a door and talked to one of the crew members.

3. Later that afternoon, Edna was taking her wet clothes to the laundry room.

She automatically arranged the flowers.

4. What word means **without thinking?**

5. What word means that she put things where she wanted them?

6. Captain Parker's ship passed through a place where hundreds of ships have sunk or been lost. Name that place.

7. Two things happen to melted rock when it moves down the sides of a volcano. Name those 2 things.

8. The picture shows marks left by an animal. Which arrow shows the direction the animal is moving?

9. Write the letter of the part that shows the mark left by the animal's tail.

10. Write the letter of the part that shows a footprint.

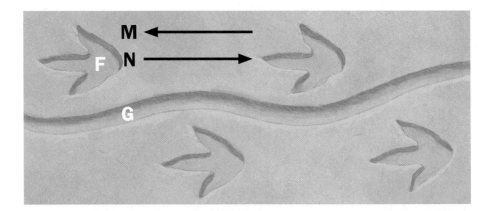

11. The earth makes a circle around the sun one time every ⬛ .

12. How many days does it take the earth to make one full circle around the sun?

13. How many heat lines are hitting place R on the map?

14. How many heat lines are hitting place A?

15. How many heat lines are hitting place M?

16. Write the letter of the place that's the hottest.

17. Write the letter of the place that's the coldest.

18. Write the letter of the place that has the warmest winters.

19. Write the letter of the place that's the farthest from the equator.

20. Why is place M hotter than place R?

21. During winter at the North Pole, how much does the sun shine?

   • never   • all the time

22. During summer at the North Pole, how much does the sun shine?

   • never   • all the time

END OF LESSON 35

A

1

1. arrange
2. magazine
3. material
4. Esther
5. electricity
6. expression

2

1. possible
2. everyone
3. grandmother
4. automobile
5. display
6. exhibit

3

1. embarrassed
2. embarrassing
3. actually
4. hurrying
5. pencils
6. crazier

4

1. invent
2. invention
3. pace
4. character
5. Leonard
6. museum
7. speech

5

1. darted
2. recorders
3. marched
4. freezer
5. chewed
6. outing

Inventing

You live in a world that is filled with things that are made by humans. In this world are cars and airplanes and telephones and books. There are chairs and tables and stoves and dishes. There are thousands of things that you use every day.

Each of these things was invented. That means that somebody made the object for the first time. The person who made the first automobile invented the automobile. The person who made the first television invented the television. Remember, when somebody makes an object for the first time, the person invents that object. The object the person makes is called the invention. The first airplane was an invention. The first telephone was an invention.

Everything that is made by humans was invented by somebody. At one time, there were no cars, light bulbs, or glass windows. People didn't know how to make these things, because nobody had invented them yet.

Most of the things that you use every day were invented after the year 1800. Here are just some of the things that people did not have before 1800: trains, trucks, cars, airplanes, bicycles, telephones, radios, televisions, movies, cell phones, computers, electric appliances like washing machines, toasters, refrigerators, or dishwashers.

Leonard the Inventor
Grandmother Esther

The year was 1980. Leonard was 12 years old. He was at the museum with his grandmother. Going places with Grandmother Esther was fun, but it was also embarrassing. It was embarrassing because Grandmother Esther had a lot to say, and she talked in a very loud voice. She talked the loudest and the longest about inventing. So when Leonard went to the museum with Grandmother Esther, he was ready to hear a lot of loud talk about inventing.

In the museum, they spent a little time looking at the displays of wild animals and the dinosaurs.

Leonard wanted to spend more time here, but Grandmother Esther kept hurrying Leonard along. She would say, "Let's keep moving or we won't see all the things we want to look at in the other parts of the museum."

Leonard knew what parts of the museum his grandmother was talking about—the displays of the first automobiles, the first airplanes, the first computers, and other things, such as the first radios.

So Grandmother Esther swept Leonard through the display of Egypt 4 thousand years ago. She darted through the exhibit of the cave people and through the display of horses. She slowed her pace as the two approached the display of the first airplanes.

As they walked through the large doorway of the exhibit hall, she announced, "Here is where we see the work of the most important people in the world—the inventors."

Leonard listened to his grandmother's speech about inventors. He nodded and very quietly said, "Yes." He was hoping that she might talk more softly if he talked softly, so he spoke in a voice that was almost a whisper. But it didn't work. Grandmother Esther's voice echoed across the large display hall.

"Without inventors there would be nothing," she said. Other people were starting to look at her and Leonard. Leonard could feel his ears getting hot from embarrassment.

"Where would we be today without inventors?" she asked herself loudly. ★ Then she answered her own question: "We would have no planes because nobody would invent them. We would have no electric lights, no radios. We would not be able to build buildings like this one. We would still be living in caves!"

Grandmother Esther said the word **caves** so loudly that a guard at the other end of the exhibit hall turned around and stared at her. Grandmother Esther marched to the display of the first airplane and pointed to it. "This was a great invention," she announced. "The two men who invented it knew that a machine could fly through the air. But other people didn't believe them. They said the inventors were crazy for working on a flying machine. But the inventors didn't give up. They invented a machine that actually flew. Once others saw that it was possible for machines to fly, they began inventing better flying machines. They invented faster machines and bigger machines. Look at them!" She waved her arm in the direction of the other airplanes on display. Nearly everyone in the hall looked at the rows of planes.

Grandmother Esther marched down the center aisle of the display. In a great voice, she said, "But none of these later planes would be

possible without the first one. And the first one would not have been possible without the inventors—those brave inventors who didn't listen to other people but who <u>knew</u> that we <u>don't</u> have to stand with our feet stuck in the mud. We can <u>fly</u> with the <u>birds</u>!"

The sound of her voice echoed through the hall. Then, one of the people who had been listening to her began to clap. Then others clapped. Soon there was a loud sound of clapping. Even the guard was clapping. Leonard was very embarrassed, but he didn't want to be the only one not clapping. So he clapped, too. He said to himself, "My grandmother is a real character."

Number your paper from 1 through 18.

 D SKILL ITEMS

Write the word from the box that means the same thing as the underlined part of each sentence.

adventure	enormous	however	hardened
approached	displayed	mysterious	glanced

1. The ice cream <u>became hard</u> in the freezer.

2. He went to school, <u>but</u> he was sick.

3. She <u>looked quickly</u> at the sign.

Use the words in the box to write complete sentences that you have learned.

| actually | exhibit | directed | automatically |
| character | displayed | divided | arranged |

4. The new ▇▇ ▇▇ mysterious fish.

5. She ▇▇ ▇▇ the flowers.

E **REVIEW ITEMS**

6. Which letter shows the place that has the warmest winters?

7. Which letter shows the place that is closest to the equator?

8. Which letter shows the place that is closest to a pole?

9. Is the North Pole or the South Pole closer to that letter?

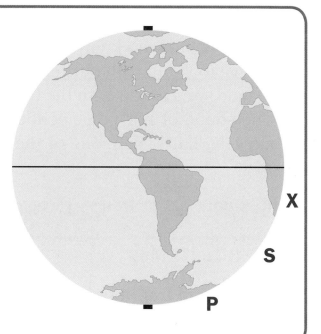

X

S

P

10. Write the letter of the earth that has the North Pole tilting away from the sun.

11. Write the letter of the earth that has the North Pole tilting toward the sun.

12. Write the letter of the earth that has darkness all around the North Pole.

13. Write the letter of the earth that has daylight all around the North Pole.

14. Write **A, B, C,** and **D.** Then write the season each earth in the picture shows.

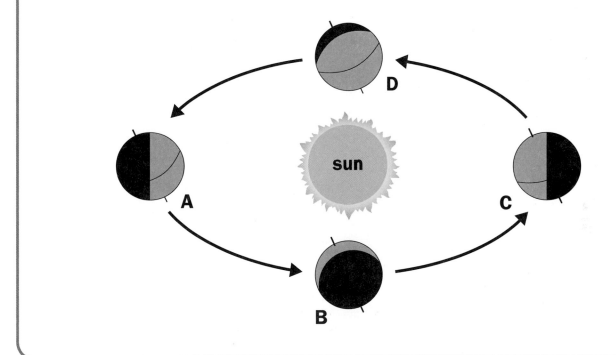

15. Two things happen to melted rock when it moves down the sides of a volcano. Name those 2 things.

16. What is it called when the earth shakes and cracks?

17. Most of the things that we use every day were invented after the year ⬛ .

- 1900   • 2000   • 1800

18. Write the letters of the 5 things that were not invented by anybody.

a. horses   f. bushes

b. buildings   g. doors

c. flowers   h. cows

d. snakes   i. wagons

e. shoes   j. hats

A

1

1. sharp-minded
2. exhibit
3. hard-boiled
4. myself

2

1. outdoors
2. railroad
3. stairway
4. understand
5. waterbed

3

1. arranged
2. crazier
3. choked
4. stuffed
5. coughed
6. expression

4

1. material
2. electricity
3. magazine
4. invention
5. inventors

5

1. automatic
2. figures
3. noticing
4. ceiling

Grandmother Esther's Inventions

Leonard and his grandmother had been in the museum all morning. Now they were sitting outdoors, on the wide stairway that led from the museum. Grandmother Esther was pulling things from her lunch bag and setting them on the stair, as she talked and continued talking. Leonard thought that she would never stop.

"Yes," she said, "I was an inventor myself." Leonard had heard this story so many times that he could say the whole thing as well as she could.

"Yes," she repeated, "but things were different back then. Nobody wanted to pay attention to a <u>woman</u> inventor. Everybody used to believe that inventors were a crazy bunch anyhow. But they thought that a <u>woman</u> inventor had to be even crazier than the other inventors. So nobody listened to me, and so some great inventions were never made."

She took a bite from a hard-boiled egg. Leonard thought she might stop talking while she ate, but she talked with her mouth full. "Yes," she said. "I actually invented the first waterbed years before anybody else did. But you couldn't get good material back then, so it leaked a little bit, and everybody said it was a crazy idea."

She continued, "I also invented a bicycle that you could fold up and carry with you. Just because there were a few little problems with it, people thought it was crazy. But they didn't understand that I could have fixed those problems. With just a little more work, I could have made a bike that wouldn't fold up when you were riding it."

Leonard wanted to invent things, too, but he couldn't figure out what to invent. Almost without thinking, he said, "Well, the trouble with being an inventor is that everything has already been invented."

Grandmother Esther started to cough with egg in her mouth. While she was still coughing, she said, "Leonard, what kind of talk is that?" She pointed to the large hall behind her and continued, "Think of how the world looked to people a hundred years ago. They said, 'We've got horse carts and buildings, and we have railroads and ships, so we must have everything. ★ There is nothing more to invent.' But a few sharp-minded people could see that people didn't have everything."

Leonard realized that she was right. The people who lived in caves probably thought that everything had been invented. They didn't know about radios and automobiles and planes and television.

Grandmother Esther was still talking as she ate her sandwich. "Remember that the inventor sees things that are not there yet; the inventor thinks about how things could be. Everybody else just sees things as they are now."

Leonard nodded his head, and for a moment he thought about what she said. Then he asked, "But how do you think about things that haven't been invented? What do you do, just think of make-believe things?"

She coughed and then she shouted, "Inventors deal in what people need, not make-believe. That's where the invention starts—looking around and noticing that people have trouble doing some things. The inventor sees a need that people have." Grandmother Esther paused and stuffed the rest of her sandwich in her mouth. In an instant, she continued, "After the inventor sees a need, the inventor figures out how to meet that need."

"I don't understand," Leonard said.

She pointed back toward the exhibit hall and said, "The two men who invented the airplane saw a need—they saw that people could get places faster if they could fly in a straight line rather than traveling around on roads. They said to themselves, 'Let's make something that will let people go places faster.' And after a lot more thinking and work, they invented a flying machine."

She continued, "The person who invented the car saw a need. That person saw that horses were a lot of work and people spent a lot of time feeding them and taking care of them. With a car, people would save time two ways: they could go faster from place to place and they wouldn't have to take care of horses."

She pointed her finger at Leonard and continued, "Remember, if you want to be an inventor, start with a need; then figure out how to meet that need."

Number your paper from 1 through 21.

C REVIEW ITEMS

1. Write the letters of the 3 things you find in the Bermuda Triangle.

   a. huge waves   c. streams   e. ice floes

   b. mountains   d. whirlpools   f. sudden storms

2. The picture shows half a hailstone. How many times did the stone go through a cloud?

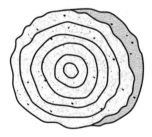

3. What is a person doing when the person makes an object for the first time?

4. The person who makes an object for the first time is called an ▆▆▆▆ .

5. The object the person makes is called an ▆▆▆▆ .

6. Write the letters of the 2 kinds of places that are safe for geese.

   a. places with a few ducks

   b. places with no geese or ducks

   c. places with a few geese

   d. places with many geese

7. Write the letter of the layer that went into the pile **first.**

8. Write the letter of the layer that went into the pile **next.**

9. Write the letter of the layer that went into the pile **last.**

10. Which layer went into the pile **earlier, B** or **C?**

11. Which layer went into the pile **earlier, D** or **C?**

12. Write the letter of the layer where we would find the skeletons of humans.

13. Write the letter of the layer that has dinosaur skeletons.

14. Write the letter of the layer where we would find the skeletons of horses.

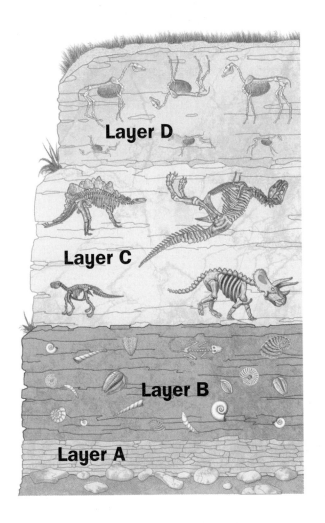

15. When days get longer, is the North Pole tilting **toward the sun** or **away from the sun?**

16. When days get shorter, is the North Pole tilting **toward the sun** or **away from the sun?**

17. In April, the sun shines for more than ▓▓▓ hours each day in Alaska.

18. Which globe shows how the earth looks on the first day of winter?

19. Which globe shows how the earth looks on the first day of summer?

Q   sun   P

20. How long ago did dinosaurs live on the earth?

- a hundred years ago

- a hundred million years ago

- a million years ago

D STUDY ITEM

21. Today's story mentions the two men who invented the first airplane. Look in a book on airplanes or on a computer and see if you can find out the names of these two men.

END OF LESSON 37

A

1	2	3
1. invisible	1. vocabulary	1. chuckled
2. suggest	2. automatically	2. ceiling
3. protection	3. remove	3. repeated
4. explanation	4. appear	4. magazine
	5. writer	5. expression

B Chapter 3

Trying to Discover Needs

Leonard tried to think like an inventor, but the job was a lot harder than Leonard thought it would be. At first, Leonard had a lot of trouble trying to figure out things that people might need. He tried to remember that Grandmother Esther had told him to start with a need and then figure out how to meet that need. But figuring out what people need was a big problem for Leonard.

Leonard started out by asking people, "What do you need?" First, he approached his father and said, "Dad, I'm thinking of inventing some things and I was wondering what you need."

His dad looked up from the paper he was reading and smiled.

"Well," his dad said as he put the paper down. "Well," he repeated, "let me see." He looked up at the ceiling and said once more, "Let me see." Suddenly Leonard's dad chuckled and said, "I could use more money, so maybe you can invent a tree that grows money."

Leonard smiled as his dad continued, "It would be nice to have less traffic on the road, so maybe you could invent a way to take traffic off the road."

Leonard didn't even smile over his dad's last idea. "Come on, Dad," he said, "I'm not kidding around. I need some ideas about things I might be able to invent, but I have to start with a <u>need</u>."

"Well, let me see," his father said, and looked down at the paper again. "There are probably a lot of things that people need, but I can't think of one right now."

"Okay," Leonard said, "thanks anyhow." To himself, he was saying, "My dad just doesn't have the mind of an inventor."

Next, Leonard talked to his mother. "Mom," he said, "I need ideas for inventions." He explained his problem to her while she was working at her desk.

"Oh, dear," she said, "every time I go somewhere I can think of a million things that would make good inventions. Let me see if I can remember something." She rubbed her chin and looked off into space as she repeated, "Let me see."

After a few moments, she said, "Oh, yes, I would like to have something that automatically made up the grocery list—you know, when the refrigerator gets low on milk, the word **milk** automatically goes on the list. ★ Or when we run out of peanut butter, **peanut butter** appears on the list."

"Yeah," Leonard said. "That sounds pretty good, but how would that work?"

His mother looked at him with a puzzled expression and said, "Leonard, I'm not the inventor. You asked if I knew of something that should be invented; you didn't ask me how to invent it. If you want to know how to invent it, go ask your grandmother."

So Leonard went to his grandmother and explained his mother's idea for an automatic grocery list. Then he said, "But I don't know how to invent an automatic list."

Grandmother Esther was reading an automobile magazine. She looked up over her glasses and shook her head no. She said, "Your mother has had that crazy idea about the automatic list for twenty years. She must have tried to get me to invent that list fifty times. And I must have told her five thousand times that I don't know how to invent a list that automatically writes down things when you get low on them. But every time I turn around, here she is again, talking about that same invention. I think your mother's problem is that she hates to go grocery shopping and she doesn't like to make up grocery lists. Now I'm not saying that it's impossible to invent something that would make up lists; I'm just saying that you're looking at one inventor who doesn't know how to do it."

"Okay," Leonard said, "thanks anyhow."

As he left the room, Grandmother Esther continued looking at her magazine, and saying to herself, "Again and again and again I kept telling her, I don't know how to do it. But she kept coming back with the same idea, that silly automatic list writer."

During the week that followed, Leonard talked to nearly everybody about things they thought should be invented. At the end of the week, he didn't have any good ideas for inventions, but he had discovered something important—people just don't seem to be very good at telling about things that they need. Leonard said to himself, "Maybe the hardest part of being an inventor is finding something to invent."

Number your paper from 1 through 24.

C SKILL ITEMS

They were impressed by her large vocabulary.

1. What word means they thought her vocabulary was very good?

2. What word refers to all the words a person knows?

3. The men who invented the first airplane saw a need. What need?

4. Write the letter of the footprint made by the heaviest animal.

5. Write the letter of the footprint made by the lightest animal.

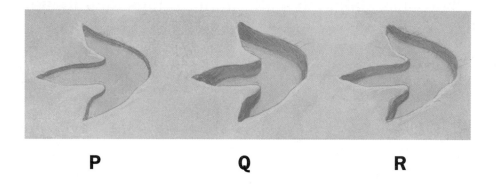

P　　　　**Q**　　　　**R**

The picture shows marks left by an animal.

6. Which arrow shows the direction the animal is moving?

7. Write the letter of the part that shows a footprint.

8. Write the letter of the part that shows the mark left by the animal's tail.

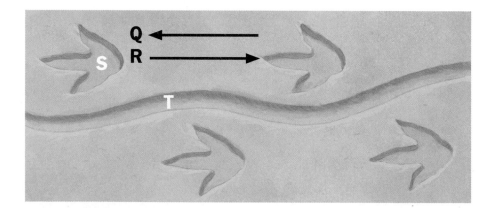

9. Geese live in large groups called ▮▮▮▮ .

10. Where are most wild geese born?

11. In which direction do geese fly in the fall?

12. What is this trip called?

13. The ▮▮▮▮s are the coldest places on the earth, and the ▮▮▮▮ is the hottest place on the earth.

14. Which letter shows the part of the earth that receives more heat from the sun than any other part?

15. Which letter shows a part of the earth that receives less heat from the sun than any other part?

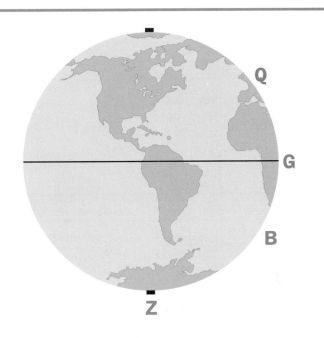

16. If you can see the sun, is it **daytime** or **nighttime** on your side of the earth?

17. What is it on the other side of the earth?

18. The earth turns around one time every ▮▮▮▮ hours.

19. Write the letter of the earth that shows the person in daytime.

20. Write the letter of the earth that shows the person 6 hours later.

21. Write the letter that shows the person another 6 hours later.

22. Write the letter that shows the person another 6 hours later.

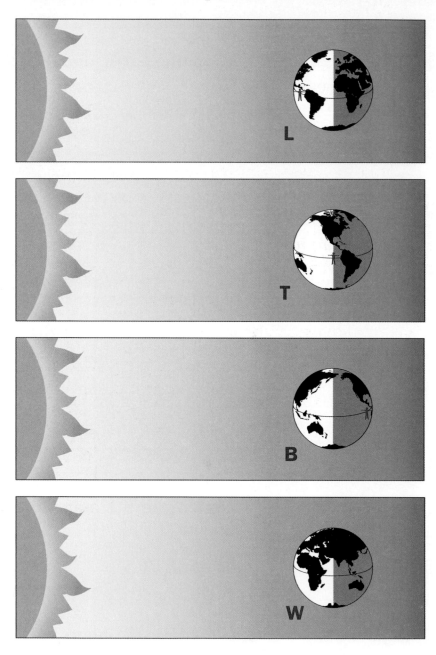

23. Write the letters of the 2 kinds of places that are safe for geese.

   a. places with many geese

   b. places with a few geese

   c. places with a few ducks

   d. places with no geese or ducks

E **STUDY ITEM**

24. The two-wheeled bicycle is not very old. It was probably hard for somebody to get the idea of a two-wheeled bicycle because it seemed impossible for somebody to move along on two wheels without falling over. Find out when J. K. Starley invented his two-wheeled *Ariel* bicycle.

END OF LESSON 38

A

1
1. assignment
2. solution
3. arithmetic
4. empty
5. electricity

2
1. <u>collar</u>
2. <u>muddy</u>
3. <u>pedal</u>
4. <u>subtract</u>
5. <u>invisible</u>
6. <u>pumpkin</u>

3
1. Frank
2. mess
3. Rita
4. Sarah
5. towels

4
1. checking
2. checker
3. tracking
4. washer
5. suggested

B   Chapter 4

Bad Ideas

Leonard had tried asking people about things that they thought he could invent. But the people he asked weren't very good about giving him good ideas. One of Leonard's friends, Frank, suggested inventing a vacation that lasted all year long. Another friend, Teddy, wanted a machine that made ice cream from dirt. Ann wanted something to put on her teeth so she would never have to brush them.

Rita wanted a pair of wings so she could fly. Sarah wanted something that would make her invisible. Freddie wanted a bicycle that you didn't have to pedal. You'd just sit on the thing and it would take you places. All these people had ideas about things that they wanted, but most of these ideas were dreams.

"Dreams are a problem," Grandmother Esther told Leonard. He had just told her that he was thinking about giving up the idea of being an inventor. And he had told her why. "Yes, dreams are a problem," she repeated. "Here's why, young man. There are dreams that are wishes. And there are dreams that an inventor has. The line between these dreams is not always clear." Grandmother Esther continued, "Think of the men who invented the first plane. They had a dream, a crazy dream. They wanted to fly. Men with legs who had stood on the ground from the time they were born wanted to fly with the birds. That was a dream as crazy as the dream of becoming invisible or the dream of making ice cream from dirt. And I can't help you out. You'll have to find out which dreams are just empty wishes and which dreams may turn into inventions."

She pointed her finger at him and said, "What that means, Leonard, is that you dream, but you must keep your head out of the clouds. Is that clear?"

"I think so," he said, but he wasn't sure. He turned and he left the room.

Grandmother Esther was talking to herself about dreams. "Where would we be without dreams? The inventor must have them. And who is to say that a dream is crazy? ★ It was a crazy dream to have lights that ran by electricity or machines that could add and subtract. It was a crazy dream to . . ."

⚙ Leonard was ready to forget about being an inventor. But then something happened that changed the way he looked at the problem. As he walked into the kitchen, he noticed that he had mud on the bottom of his shoes. He hadn't noticed it before. Now it was too late. He had made tracks all over the house. If only he had noticed that his shoes were dirty. For a moment, he felt very dumb for tracking mud all over the house. He could almost hear what his mother was going to say: "You should always check your shoes before coming into the house."

Leonard tiptoed over to the outside door and took off his ⚙ muddy shoes. He got some paper towels and started to clean up the mess. Then, when he had almost cleaned the last footprint on the kitchen floor, an idea hit him. It hit him so hard that it put a smile on his face. Just like that, he knew how to think like an inventor. He said out loud, "I need a shoe checker. I know I need it because when I don't have one, I don't do a good job of checking my shoes."

A shoe checker wasn't a bad idea for an invention. But the idea wasn't the most important thing to Leonard. The way he got the idea was the important thing. He didn't do something well. Then he figured out that he needed something to help him do it well.

That's how to figure out things to invent. You don't ask people. You do things. And when you do them, you pay attention to problems that you have. Each of the problems that you have tells you about something that you could invent to solve the problem.

Leonard's mother walked into the kitchen and saw Leonard smiling. "This is the first time I've seen you have a good time while you clean up a mess," she said.

"That's because I like this mess," Leonard said.

His mother shook her head. "He's a chip off the old block—just like his grandmother."

Number your paper from 1 through 20.

C SKILL ITEMS

Here are three events that happened in the story.

Write **beginning, middle,** or **end** for each event.

1. Leonard's mother walked into the kitchen and saw Leonard smiling.

2. Grandmother Esther was talking to herself about dreams.

3. One of Leonard's friends, Frank, suggested inventing a vacation that lasted all year long.

Use the words in the box to write complete sentences that you have learned.

impressed	arranged	honestly	stuffed
repeated	automatically	stomach	vocabulary

4. She ▮▮▮ ▮▮▮ the flowers.

5. They were ▮▮▮ by her large ▮▮▮ .

D REVIEW ITEMS

6. The first thing you do when you think like an inventor is find a ▮▮▮ .

7. What's the next thing you do?

8. Geese live in large groups called ▢ .

9. Where are most wild geese born?

10. In which direction do geese fly in the fall?

11. What is this trip called?

Choose from these words to answer items 12–14:

- moon
- Florida
- sun
- equator

- geese
- poles
- Canada
- migration

12. The heat that the earth receives comes from the ▢ .

13. The part of the earth that receives more heat than any other part is the ▢ .

14. The parts of the earth that receive less heat than any other part are called the ▢ .

15. The sun shines ▢ .

- some of the time
- all of the time

16. Can you see the sun all day long and all night long?

17. Things closer to the bottom of the pile went into the pile ▢ .

18. Write the letter of the storm clouds.

19. Write the letter of the clouds that may stay in the sky for days at a time.

20. Write the letter of the clouds that have frozen drops of water.

A

B

C

A

1

1. cucumber
2. provide
3. invite
4. leopard
5. entrance

2

1. vegetables
2. honest
3. tomatoes
4. cover
5. single

3

1. pumpkin
2. coals
3. leaped
4. steal
5. stealing

Why Leopard Has Spots

Told by Won-Ldy Paye,
Edited by Margaret H. Lippert, Illustrated by Beth Mills

One day there was a spider. He was a great farmer. He lived in a village with a leopard and a deer. Spider had a BIG garden. He had so much food in his garden that every evening Spider would call Leopard and Deer and cook food for them.

But one day Spider went to his garden and noticed something was different. "Something is missing," he thought. Day after day things seemed to be missing.

At first he didn't care, because his garden was so big. But then it began to make him mad. One day he looked at his garden and said, "I saw a pumpkin here last night. Why is the pumpkin not here this morning?"

The next day he said, "I thought I saw a big cucumber here. Why is it not there?"

Spider began to check his farm very carefully. He was sure there were 98 tomatoes. But when he came back, there were 95. Man, this was really getting to Spider! He told his friends that his tomatoes were missing, but they laughed at him.

"You want to tell me I'm not able to count right?" Spider asked.

Spider began to mark every single thing in his garden. Sometimes when he checked, instead of going from 1-2-3-4, the numbers went 1-3-5-7. And Spider said, "Something must be wrong!"

Spider went to Deer's hut. "Are you the one who is stealing from my garden all the time?"

Deer went: "Oh, no, no, no, no, no, no, no. Not me. You call for me every evening. You provide me dinner. Why should I go steal from your garden?"

Spider said, "I don't like stealing. I hope it's not you."

Deer said, "It's not me."

Spider went to Leopard. "Leopard, please be honest with me. Are you stealing from my garden?"

Leopard said, "No, I like meats. I really don't like too much veg-e-table. I am only eating veg-e-tables because you invite us to eat with you. You provide it for us."

Spider said, "Okay."

The vegetables kept on disappearing. Spider started to get really mad.

Spider went to Deer's house again. "Are you the one who's stealing from my garden?"

Deer said, "N-n-n-n-n-n-n-no!"

Spider said, "How come you're going 'n-n-no' like that?"

Deer said, "B-b-b-b-but that's the w-w-w-way I t-t-t-t-talk."

Spider said, "What! How come you don't talk like that all the time?"

Deer said, "When I'm m-m-m-m-mad, I t-t-t-t-talk like this." So Deer started pretending that he was mad, and that's why he was talking like this. Spider was really surprised because he never heard Deer talk like this before.

The Spider went back to Leopard's house. "Are you the one who is stealing from my garden?"

Leopard said, "I told you I like meat. I don't like veg-e-table too much. So go ask Deer."

This time when Spider came to Deer, Deer said, "Here's what you should do: Go and dig a big hole in front of the entrance to the garden, and put a lot of fire in it and build it up. Cover it with a lot of dry branches. Let the fire burn way down. When the person who is stealing from your garden goes through the entrance, they'll fall in the fire. The next day when you come, you will see them."

So Spider went and dug the hole, and lit a fire in the bottom of it. He let the fire burn way down to red-hot coals, and then he covered the hole with dry branches, just as Deer said.

But Deer knew where the hole was, because Deer was the one who told Spider the trick. So Deer went around the hole and went into Spider's garden and stole other things. Then he ran to Leopard's house, and he said, "Spider called you."

Leopard said, "Where's Spider?"

Deer said, "Spider is in his garden."

So Leopard ran to the garden. When he went through the entrance to the garden, Leopard fell in the hole. And Leopard started to get burned.

Deer ran to Spider. Deer said, "Come! Come! Come! Come! I saw the person who is stealing from the garden all the time. We should keep this old Leopard down there fighting and trying to get up."

Spider shouted to Leopard: "You've been stealing from my garden all the time! Now I've got you."

Leopard said, "I don't know what you're talking about. I just want to get out of this fire."

Spider said, "Why have you been lying to me all the time? Every time you said you are not the one. Now my trap has caught you."

Leopard said, "I don't know what you're talking about. I just want to get out of this fire."

So Leopard leaped high. Ahhh, he got out of the fire. So Leopard said, "What is all this about?"

Spider said, "Deer told me I should play this trick. And now I find out who's been stealing."

And Leopard said, "But how come Deer came to me and said that you called me to the garden?"

Spider looked at Deer and said, "Did I send you to go get Leopard?"

The Deer said, "No."

Spider said, "Ohhhh, so it's you, Deer, who's been stealing from the garden all the time."

Leopard said, "WHAT! You did that! You did this to me? Because of your trick, I've got all these black spots on my skin because I got burned in the fire!"

Since that day, all the leopards we see have black, black, black spots all over their skin.

"You did this, Deer? Because of these black spots, anywhere I see you," Leopard said, "I'M GOING TO EAT YOU!" So Deer ran away. And Leopard ran after him.

Since that day, no matter how much you train the deer, no matter how much you train the leopard, don't put them together, because Leopard is sure going to eat Deer.

That's why Deer and Leopard aren't friends now, and that's why Leopard has black spots all over his skin.

A

1

1. example
2. energy
3. device
4. agreement
5. attorney
6. patent
7. reacted

2

1. <u>when</u>ever
2. <u>shop</u>keeper
3. <u>ear</u>muffs
4. <u>bed</u>time
5. <u>bath</u>tub

3

1. impressed
2. forgetting
3. explanation
4. buzzer
5. automatically
6. umbrellas

4

1. mentioned
2. sternly
3. matching
4. protection
5. unfolded
6. bakery

5

1. collar
2. difficult
3. hood
4. plastic
5. raise
6. vocabulary
7. respond

B   Chapter 5

A Plan for Inventing

Thinking like an inventor was difficult for Leonard until he figured out this plan: He did different things. And he noticed each time he had a problem. When he noticed a problem, he knew that he had a <u>need</u>. He needed something that would solve that problem. The thing he needed to solve the problem was an invention.

After Leonard worked out his plan for finding needs, he tried to do all kinds of things. He washed the car, washed the windows, and washed the dog. He washed the floors and the walls and the dishes. He helped his dad fix a table. He helped the man who lived next door change a tire on his car.

All the time Leonard did these things, his mind was working. He tried to see where he had problems. For three weeks he did things and noticed the problems that he had. And at the end of three weeks, he had a big list of things that he might invent. Some of the ideas were pretty good.

Leonard had found out that he wasn't very good at cracking raw eggs, and he thought of an invention that would crack egg shells. Leonard had found out that he was always forgetting to hang up his clothes when he took them off at night. Then his mother would come in and say, "Leonard, Leonard, look at your clothes, all over the place." Leonard figured out that what he needed was a recording that would come on just before bedtime. The voice on the recording would say, "Leonard, Leonard, hang up your clothes. Don't just drop them under your nose."

Leonard had a problem each time it rained. Leonard hated umbrellas, so he never took one with him. But then he would be caught in the rain without an umbrella. He would get soaked.

He thought of a way to meet his need for some protection from the rain. Why not invent a coat that has a special hood? When the hood is not being used, it looks like a big collar. But when the hood is unfolded, it becomes a little umbrella. ⭐

Leonard discovered that he had a great problem when he tried to wash his dog. The problem was that Leonard got all wet. If he tried to wash the dog in the bathtub, the dog would jump out in the middle of the bath and shake. The room would then be covered with water. Leonard would then have to spend a lot of time cleaning up the mess. If Leonard washed the dog outside, the problem was not as great, but Leonard still got soaked.

He thought of an invention to meet this need. The invention was a large plastic box with holes in it. First you would fill a tub with water. Then you'd put the dog in the tub. Next, you'd put the plastic box over the tub. The dog would stick its head out through one of the holes. You could reach through the other holes and wash the dog and you wouldn't get wet while you were washing the dog. "Not bad," Leonard said to himself when he got this idea. "Not bad at all."

Leonard made pictures of some of his ideas. He showed them to the members of his family and he explained how they worked. His father said, "Leonard, I'm impressed."

Leonard's mother said, "Leonard, those are very good ideas. But did you ever think of inventing a machine that would automatically write out the things that you need at the grocery store?"

When Leonard's mother mentioned the list-making machine, Grandmother Esther said, "Stop talking about that crazy invention. Leonard seems to have some good ideas here. They show that the boy has been thinking like an inventor. Now he needs to stop thinking and start inventing." She looked sternly at Leonard.

Leonard smiled and said, "But I still don't know which thing I should invent."

"They're all pretty good," his father said.

His mother said, "I like the machine that makes up a list of things to buy."

Leonard said, "I'm not sure I've found the right idea yet."

Leonard shook his head. He was becoming very tired of trying to be an inventor.

C REVIEW ITEMS

1. What are clouds made of?

2. What kind of cloud does the picture show?

3. What happens to a drop of water at **B?**

4. At which letter would the winters be very, very hot?

5. At which letter would the winters be very, very cold?

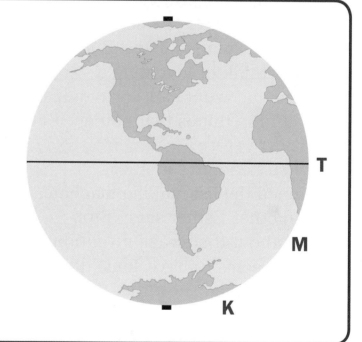

6. Female animals fight in the spring to protect ▩ .

7. Name 2 kinds of Alaskan animals that are dangerous in the spring.

8. Name 3 animals that are cold-blooded.

9. Name 3 animals that are warm-blooded.

10. Which object went into the pile **first?**

11. Which object went into the pile **earlier,** the book or the pencil?

12. Which object went into the pile **just after** the knife?

13. What kind of animals lived in the Mesozoic?

Use these names to answer the questions: **Tyrannosaurus, Triceratops.**

14. What is animal **A?**

15. What is animal **B?**

A

B

END OF LESSON 41

A

1

1. <u>in</u>terest
2. <u>a</u>side
3. <u>Gran</u>dma
4. <u>en</u>ergy
5. <u>won</u>derful
6. <u>a</u>greement

2

1. <u>ex</u>ample
2. <u>ex</u>pect
3. <u>ex</u>cuse
4. <u>cle</u>ver
5. <u>soun</u>ding
6. <u>re</u>spond

3

1. counter
2. kneeling
3. blocking
4. traced
5. serves
6. reacted

4

1. beam
2. dance
3. patent
4. she'd
5. target
6. attorney

The Electric Eye

Leonard was walking to school. Grandmother Esther was on her way to her dance class. The dance class was held near Leonard's school, so she was walking with him. Whenever she walked, she talked, and talked, and talked. And when she talked about inventing, she talked very loudly. Leonard knew that she wasn't shouting at him. He knew that she wasn't mad when she pointed her finger and raised her voice. He knew these things. But the other people who were walking along the street didn't know. They stopped and stared at Grandmother Esther. To them, it must have seemed that she was yelling at Leonard.

Leonard was very embarrassed, but he didn't know what to say. As she talked, Leonard thought about an invention he needed. What about a pair of thick earmuffs? If he wore them, he wouldn't be able to hear her. No, that wouldn't work. She'd just talk louder. What about a buzzer? The buzzer could buzz louder when she talked louder. If she wanted the buzzer to stop, she'd have to talk softly.

"Now there's an invention," she said, pointing to something. She and Leonard were in front of a bakery. The window was filled with things that looked so good to eat that Leonard tried not to look at them. Grandmother Esther seemed to be pointing at the door. "Yes, a very simple invention, but a very clever one."

"What invention is that?" Leonard asked.

"The electric eye, of course," she said.

Leonard didn't know what she was talking about. "The electric what?" he asked.

"The electric eye. Don't tell me you don't know what an electric eye is."

Before he could respond, she opened the door to the bakery. She pointed to a tiny light that was on one side of the door, about half a meter from the floor. "There it is," she said. "The electric eye."

"What does it do?" Leonard asked.

"It tells the shopkeeper that you're coming into the shop. ⭐ Watch." She held her hand in front of the little beam of light that came from the electric eye. As soon as she did that a buzzer sounded in the back of the bakery. "That's just what happens when you walk into the store."

She explained how the electric eye worked. The beam of light went from one side of the door to the other. As long as the beam reached a little target on the other side of the door, nothing happened. But when something got in the way of that beam of light and kept it from reaching the target, the buzzer sounded. She explained that the buzzer kept sounding as long as the beam was broken. So when somebody walked in the door, the body would stop the beam of light from reaching the target. When the body stopped the beam, the buzzer sounded. That buzzer told the shopkeeper that somebody was going through the door.

Grandmother Esther was kneeling in front of the doorway as she explained how the beam worked. Several people were trying to get into the bakery. They waited as she explained the electric eye. The shopkeeper was standing behind the counter, looking at her. When she finished her explanation of the electric eye, she said, "This is a good example of a clever invention. The electric eye is a simple invention, but it has many, many uses."

One of the people who was trying to get into the store said, "Very interesting."

The other person said, "Yes, very interesting."

The shopkeeper said, "Excuse me, could you stand aside and let these people come in?"

Leonard said, "Come on, Grandma, you're blocking the doorway."

And Grandmother Esther said, "Of course, the electric eye is not as great an invention as the airplane or the electric light. But the electric eye serves many needs."

The shopkeeper said, "Yes, it does."

Leonard said, "Come on, Grandma, I've got to go to school."

Number your paper from 1 through 25.

C SKILL ITEMS

He responded to her clever solution.

1. What word means **reacted?**

2. What word means very **smart?**

3. What word refers to solving a problem?

D REVIEW ITEMS

4. When geese learn to fly, do they start in the water or on the land?

5. They run with their ▓▓▓ out to the sides.

6. The earth is shaped like a ▓▓▓ .

7. The hottest part of the earth is called the ▓▓▓ .

- desert
- equator
- pole

8. What's the name of the spot that's at the bottom of the earth?

9. What's the name of the spot that's at the top of the earth?

10. What's the name of the line that goes around the fattest part of the earth?

11. What season is it at the North Pole when the North Pole tilts **away from** the sun?

12. What season is it at the North Pole when the North Pole tilts **toward** the sun?

Write the name of each numbered object in the picture. Choose from these names:

- kayak
- spear
- parka
- fishing pole
- sled
- sled dogs
- mukluks

20. In what season are animals most dangerous in Alaska?

21. During what season do female animals in Alaska have babies?

22. About how long are killer whales?

23. Compare the size of killer whales with the size of other whales.

24. Are killer whales fish?

25. Tell whether killer whales are **warm-blooded** or **cold-blooded.**

A

1
1. product
2. assignment
3. wonderful
4. sour
5. practicing
6. realizing

2
1. clearer
2. device
3. supper
4. outfit
5. drawings
6. enter

3
1. tone
2. arithmetic
3. stinks
4. solution
5. giggled
6. returning

B   Chapter 7

A Good Idea

The next evening, after supper, it happened, although Leonard had no warning that it would happen. Everything in his mind suddenly came together and he had the idea for a wonderful invention.

Here's how it happened: After supper, he went to his room to get a pencil so he could make some more drawings of ideas for inventions. When he was returning to the kitchen, Grandmother Esther hollered at him, "Turn off the light in your room. Remember you're supposed to save energy."

Leonard turned around, returned to his bedroom, turned off the light, and stood there in the darkness.

He felt the idea coming into his brain and then felt it get bigger and clearer and . . . "Hot dog!" he shouted in a voice that was too loud. He shouted, "What an idea for an invention!"

He ran into the kitchen. "I've got a great idea! This is the best idea anybody ever had for an invention!"

His mother smiled and said, "I'll bet it's a machine that automatically makes up a grocery list."

"Stop talking about that machine for writing lists," Grandmother Esther yelled from the other room. She ran into the kitchen, wearing her running shoes.

Grandmother Esther asked, "What's your idea, Leonard?"

Leonard said, "Let me explain how it's going to work: It's dark outside, and it's dark in the living room of your house. But when you walk through the door to the living room, the light goes on automatically. The light stays on as long as you're in the living room, but when you leave the living room, the light goes off."

Leonard's mother shook her head and said, "That sounds far too difficult for an invention."

Grandmother Esther replied, "It sounds difficult to you because you don't know how the electric eye works."

"The electric eye?" Leonard's mother asked.

Leonard explained, "Here's how it works, Mom. There's a little beam of light that goes across the doorway to the living room. When you enter the room, you break the beam of light. When you break that beam, the light turns on; when you leave the room, you break the beam and the light goes off." ★

"Oh, my," Leonard's mother said and shook her head several times. He could tell from her tone of voice that she didn't understand his explanation.

"Good thinking," Grandmother Esther said, and slapped Leonard on the back. "That's a wonderful idea for an invention, a wonderful idea."

"Thank you," Leonard said.

Grandmother Esther made a sour looking face. Slowly she said, "There's one big problem with being a good inventor. You have to think of all the things that could go wrong with your invention."

"What could go wrong?" Leonard asked.

Grandmother Esther explained, "When you break the beam one time, the light goes on. When you break the beam the next time, the light goes off. When you break the beam the next time, the light goes on."

"Right," Leonard said as he nodded his head up and down.

"Here's the problem," Grandmother Esther said: "What if two people walk into a dark room? When the first one goes into the room, the light will turn on, but when the second person goes into the room, what happens to the light?"

"The light goes off," Leonard said very sadly and shook his head. "Now both people are in the dark, and my invention stinks."

"Wrong!" Grandmother Esther shouted. "Both people are in the dark, but your invention does not stink. Every invention has problems, but a good inventor looks at these problems and figures out how to solve them. You must remember that inventing something is more than just getting an idea; you must work on that idea until it is a good idea. Then you must take that good idea and make it into a good invention. Just because there's a problem doesn't mean that an inventor gives up. You've got a great idea, but it needs work."

Leonard's mother said, "I have a great idea for an invention. It's a machine that . . ."

"Not now," Grandmother Esther said. "We're very close to a real invention."

Leonard said, "I'll just have to think about the problem and try to figure out how to solve it."

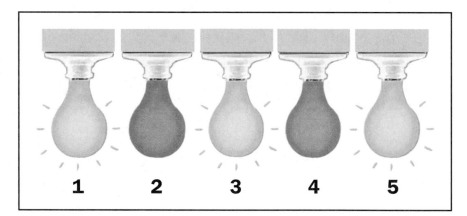

1   2   3   4   5

C SKILL ITEMS

Use the words in the box to write complete sentences you have learned.

device	outfit	solution	returning
impressed	mentioned	responded	vocabulary

1. They were ▭ by her large ▭ .
2. He ▭ to her clever ▭ .

D REVIEW ITEMS

Here's how an electric eye at a store works.

3. When somebody walks in the door, the body stops the beam of light from reaching the ▭ .

4. When the body stops the beam, what does the device do next?

5. What does that tell the shopkeeper?

6. What's the name of geese that are all white?

7. What's the name of geese that are black, brown, and white?

8. What color are all geese when they are born?

9. How old are geese when they mate for the first time?

10. After male and female geese mate, how long do they stay together?

11. Most geese live for about ▭ years.

12. Write the letter of the layer that went into the pile first.

13. Write the letter of the layer that went into the pile next.

14. Write the letter of the layer that went into the pile last.

15. Write the letter of the layer that we live on.

16. What's the name of layer **C**?

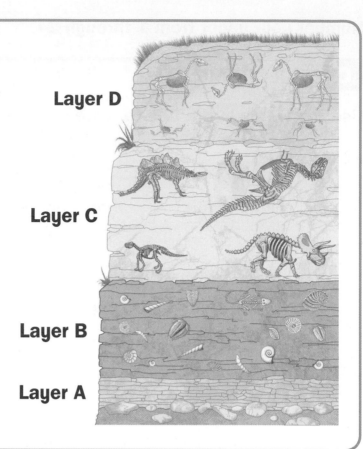

Layer D

Layer C

Layer B

Layer A

17. Name the country that is just north of the United States.

18. Which letter shows where the United States is?

19. Which letter shows where Canada is?

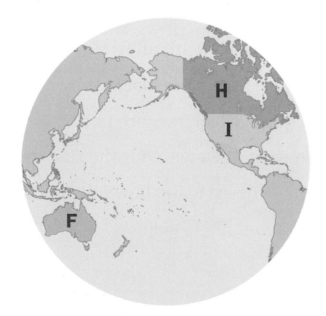

20. The picture shows half a hailstone. How many times did the stone go through a cloud?

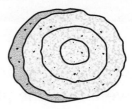

21. When geese learn to fly, do they start in the water or on the land?

22. They run with their ▆▆▆ out to the sides.

23. How many poles are there?

24. The farther you go from the equator, the ▆▆▆ you get.

- hotter   • colder   • fatter

A

1
1. <u>bath</u>room
2. <u>one</u>-way
3. <u>home</u>work
4. <u>out</u>fit
5. <u>drum</u>roll

2
1. entering
2. drums
3. practicing
4. realizing
5. gaining

3
1. shaft
2. whether
3. drew
4. goose
5. product

B   Chapter 8

One Way

Leonard said to himself, "Figure out how to solve that problem." It was a real problem. Every time the beam is broken, the lights change. If they are on, they go off. So if somebody is in a room with the lights on and somebody else comes into the room, the beam is broken and the lights go off.

He was on his way to school. He walked past the bakery. For a moment he remembered how embarrassed he had been when Grandmother Esther blocked the people who were trying to come into the store.

From time to time his mind would notice other things around him, but most of the time it was busy with the problem. "Think."

Then Leonard realized that he was looking at a sign. "One way," the sign said. And it had an arrow. "One way." Although Leonard didn't figure out the answer to his problem at that moment, he had a very strange feeling, as if he were very close to the answer. Leonard said, "My device has to know which way you are going. It has to know if you are entering the room or leaving the room." Leonard crossed the street. Then he stopped and said out loud, "But one electric eye can't tell whether you're coming in or going out."

Two boys who were walking to school giggled and pointed at Leonard. When Leonard saw them pointing, he realized how crazy he must have looked as he talked to himself.

Later that day in school, Leonard was supposed to be doing his arithmetic homework. He liked arithmetic and he was good at it, but he couldn't seem to work on it that day. He kept thinking of the problem and the one-way sign. Without realizing what he was doing, he drew the sign on his paper.

⚙ He studied the arrow. He traced it with his pencil three or four times. Then he traced over the letters in the sign. Then he put two dots next to each other on the shaft of the arrow. Suddenly, he felt goose bumps all over his arms and down his back. ★ He almost jumped out of his seat. "Wow!" he shouted. "I've got it!"

Everybody in the class was looking at him. He could feel his face becoming very hot. He cleared his throat and coughed. Then he looked down at his paper. He could still feel the eyes of everybody in the room looking at him. Then he heard the teacher's voice. "Is anything ⚙ wrong, Leonard?"

Leonard looked up. "No, no. I just figured out the solution to a problem I've been working on."

The teacher said, "I'm glad to see that you are so excited about solving your arithmetic problems, but when you work out the solution to the next problem, try to be a little more quiet about it."

• • •

After school that day, Leonard ran home. It felt great to run. Sometimes when he ran he felt heavy, but as he went home that afternoon, he felt very light and very fast. He could feel the wind on his face. He raced with the cars when they started out from stop signs. He could stay with them for more than half a city block.

When he got home, he ran into the house. "Grandma!" he shouted. "I've got it!" Grandmother Esther was practicing on her drums. Leonard's mother was in the hall. She was wearing earmuffs.

Leonard told Grandmother Esther how to solve the problem. "On the side of the door we put two electric eyes, not one." Leonard continued, "The electric eyes are side by side. When somebody goes through the door, they will break one beam first, then the second beam. If the outside beam is broken first and the inside beam is broken next, the person is moving <u>into</u> the room."

Leonard continued to explain, "If the inside beam is broken first and the outside beam is broken next, the person is moving <u>out</u> of the room. We make the electric eye device turn on the light if somebody goes <u>into</u> the room and turn <u>off</u> the light if somebody goes <u>out</u> of the room."

Grandmother Esther smiled and said,"Now you're gaining ground on being an inventor."

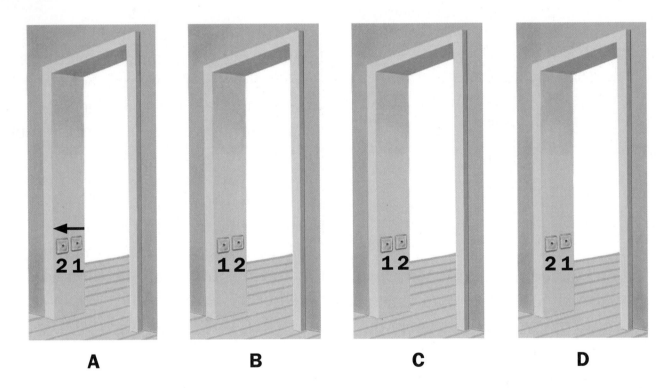

A   B   C   D

Number your paper from 1 through 28.

C STORY ITEMS

1. In today's story, what was Leonard doing that made two boys on the street giggle and point at him?

2. What did Leonard do when he figured out the solution?

3. Where was he?

4. When Leonard got home, his mother was wearing earmuffs. Why?

5. How many electric eyes will Leonard need on each doorway?

6. How many beams will go across the doorway?

7. Leonard's first invention had problems. Let's say two people walk into a dark room. What happens to the light in the room when the first person enters?

8. What happens to the light when the second person enters?

D REVIEW ITEMS

9. Which came earlier on the earth, dinosaurs or horses?

10. Which came earlier on the earth, strange sea animals or dinosaurs?

11. What's the name of the place shown by the letter **C?**

12. Which letter shows the hottest place?

13. Which letter shows the coldest place?

14. Which letter is farthest from the equator?

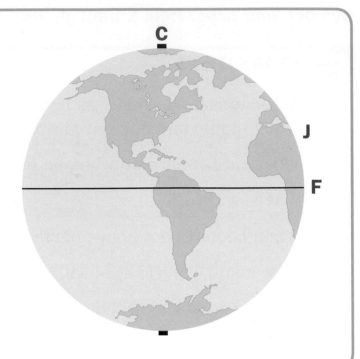

15. What are clouds made of?

16. What kind of cloud does the picture show?

17. What happens to a drop of water at **B?**

18. Most geese live for about [   ] years.

19. How old are geese when they mate for the first time?

20. After male and female geese mate, how long do they stay together?

21. Which letter shows the place that is closest to the equator?

22. Which letter shows the place that is closest to a pole?

23. Is the **North Pole** or the **South Pole** closer to that letter?

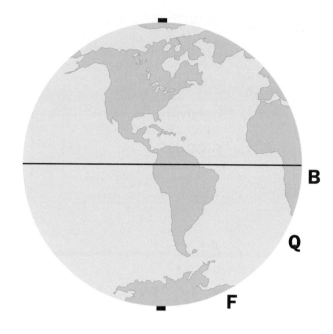

24. Name 2 things that can make an ice chunk drift.

E STUDY ITEMS

Grandmother Esther talked about what a great invention the electric light bulb is. The man who invented it was named Thomas Alva Edison.

25. Find out when he invented the electric light bulb.

26. Find out 2 other things that he invented.

27. Margaret E. Knight was known as a "woman Edison." In what year did she invent a machine to make grocery store paper bags?

28. Find out 2 things she invented.

A

1
1. diagram
2. lawyer
3. purchase
4. attorney
5. permission
6. electrical

2
1. secret
2. rapped
3. shame
4. booming
5. product

3
1. snappy
2. sighed
3. company
4. patent
5. drumroll

B Chapter 9

Another Problem

"That's a great solution," Grandmother Esther said. Leonard had just explained his idea. Instead of one electric eye on the side of the door, he would use two of them. When somebody walked into the room, the body would break one beam before the other beam. If the outside beam was broken first, the person was moving into the room. If the inside beam was broken first, the person was moving out of the room.

Leonard explained, "As soon as I saw that arrow on the one-way sign, I knew that I was close to the solution."

"Good job," Grandmother Esther said and rapped out a snappy drumroll. Grandmother Esther continued, "But there is still one problem."

"Oh, no," Leonard said. "Not another problem."

Grandmother Esther hit the biggest drum. Then she said, "Your machine can tell whether somebody comes into the room or goes out of the room. And your machine turns off the lights when somebody leaves the room."

Then she said, "But what would happen if three people were sitting in the room reading and one of them left the room?"

Leonard sighed and said, "The light would go off."

Leonard felt dumb for not seeing this problem before his grandmother pointed it out. The electric eye device that he had imagined couldn't count. It couldn't tell if one person was in the room or if ten were in the room. The only thing Leonard's device knew how to do was to turn the lights on if somebody came into the room and turn them off if somebody left the room. But the device didn't know how many people were in the room.

Grandmother Esther said, "Your invention has to know how to count people in the room." Then she made a long drumroll and ended it with a terribly loud boom. "So, make it count," she said.

"How do I do that?" Leonard asked.

She responded, "What if you had a counter on your device? When a person went into the room, the counter would count one. When the next person went into the room, the counter would count again—two. With a counter, your device would know how many people are in the room. It wouldn't shut off the lights until the last person left the room."

For a few moments, Leonard thought about what she said. Then he said, "I get it. The lights wouldn't go off if there were still some people in the room." Then he added, "But I don't know how to make the device count."

"Think, think, think," she said and began to tap on the smallest drum. "Think, Leonard, think," she repeated.

Leonard knew that she wasn't going to tell him any more about how to make the device count, so he left the room and began to think.

For nearly the rest of the day, Leonard's mind kept hearing his grandmother say, "Think, think, think." But the problem was much harder for Leonard than she made it sound. He thought and thought.

Just before supper, he went into the bathroom. He filled the sink with water and washed his hands. When he started to let the water out of the sink, he got the idea. The water would keep going out of the sink until the sink was empty. The water kept going out until there was <u>zero</u> water in the sink. That was the secret. "Count to zero," he said out loud.

He ran to his room and got some paper. Then he made a little drawing that showed how the device could count. Look at the drawing that he made.

Leonard ran into the kitchen. Grandmother Esther was starting to eat her salad. He showed her the drawing and explained. "The device can tell each time somebody goes into the room and each time somebody goes out. So we make a counter that counts <u>forward</u> each time somebody goes into the room. If four people go into the room, the counter counts one, two, three, four. Each time somebody leaves the room, the counter counts <u>backward</u>. So if three people leave, the counter counts backward: three, two, one. But the lights don't go off until the counter counts back to zero."

Leonard continued to explain, "When the last person leaves the room, the counter counts back to zero. Now the lights go off."

Grandmother Esther jumped out of her chair, threw her arms around Leonard, and gave him a kiss.

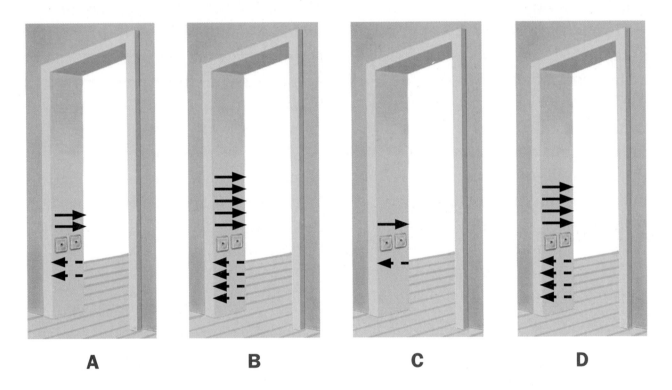

A   B   C   D

Number your paper from 1 through 25.

C STORY ITEMS

1. How many electric eyes did Leonard use for his invention?

2. How many beams went across the doorway?

3. If a person moves into a room, which beam will be broken first—the inside beam or the outside beam?

4. Which beam will be broken next?

5. The solid arrows show how many times people went into the room. How many people went into the room?

6. The dotted arrow shows how many people left the room. How many people left the room?

7. Are the lights on in the room?

8. How many more people would have to leave the room before the lights go off?

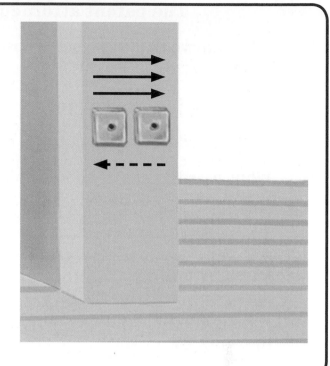

D SKILL ITEMS

Here are the three events that happened in the chapter.
Write **beginning, middle,** or **end** for each event.

9. The water kept going out until there was zero water in the sink.

10. Leonard told Grandmother Esther that the one-way sign helped him figure out a solution.

11. Leonard told his Grandmother Esther how the counter on his device would work.

The patent attorney wrote an agreement.

12. What do we call a lawyer whose special job is getting patents for new inventions?

13. What word means **lawyer?**

14. What word means a **promise made by people?**

15. What word names a license for somebody to be the only person who can make a product?

E REVIEW ITEMS

16. How many days does it take the earth to make one full circle around the sun?

17. The earth makes a circle around the sun one time every ▭ .

18. How many heat lines are hitting place **E** on the map?

19. How many heat lines are hitting place **G?**

20. How many heat lines are hitting place **J?**

21. Which letter on the map shows Canada?

22. Which letter shows Alaska?

23. Which letter shows the main part of the United States?

24. Which 2 letters show where Inuits live?

25. How warm is it during winter in Alaska?

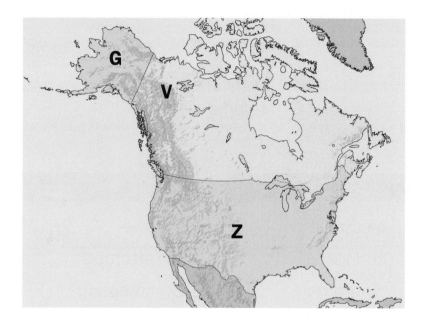

A

1
1. business
2. manufacturer
3. disappointed
4. flood
5. turner-off-er
6. ninety

2
1. model
2. patent
3. purchase
4. supply
5. automatic
6. anytime

3
1. electrical
2. connected
3. diagrams
4. lawyers
5. announcer
6. patented

4
1. owe
2. attorney
3. company
4. permission
5. phoned
6. snapping

B   Chapter 10

Leonard's Model

It's easy to say that the invention will count things, but it's a much harder job to build a device that counts. Grandmother Esther was a big help for this part of the job. She knew a lot about electricity. Grandmother Esther got books for Leonard that showed him where to buy electric eyes and how to hook electric wires up to make the electric eyes work. These books also showed where to purchase electric counters. After Leonard and his grandmother decided which type of electric eyes they wanted, she made a few phone calls, took Leonard with her in her truck, and bought the supplies that they needed to build a model of his invention.

"Now remember, Leonard," she said as they left the electrical supply store. "You owe me ninety dollars. When you start making money from your invention, just remember that I'm giving up my fishing trip so that you can build your invention."

"You shouldn't give up your fishing trip, Grandmother," he said. "I'll get the money."

"I'm kidding you," she said. "I'd much rather invent something than go fishing anytime." She started up the truck and made the engine roar loudly. Suddenly, the truck jumped forward, snapping Leonard's head back. And off they went to their home.

Leonard and his grandmother built a model of the electric eye device. The model was a little room with a doorway that was about one meter tall. There was a light bulb connected to the top of the doorway.

To show how the model worked, Leonard used a large teddy bear and large dolls. Leonard moved these objects through the doorway. An object would break the outside beam first, then the inside beam. As soon as the first object broke both beams, the light went on. Leonard would move more objects through the doorway and the light would stay on.

Then Leonard would begin to move the objects the other way. The light would stay on until the last object went back through the doorway. Then the light would go off.

"This device works!" Leonard shouted after he and his grandmother had tested it four times. ★ "It works. We've invented an automatic light turner-off-er!"

But Leonard's work was not finished. He had a model of the invention, and that model worked. But now he had to protect his invention. An invention needs protection from people who copy it and say that it is their invention. To protect an invention, the inventor gets a patent. When an invention is patented, the only person who can make copies of that invention is the inventor. If other people want to make copies of it, they have to get permission from the inventor. The inventor may tell somebody that it is all right to make copies of the invention. But the inventor doesn't usually give somebody this right. The inventor sells the right. The inventor may say this to the person who wants to make copies: "Each time you make a copy, you must give me so much money." Maybe the person has to pay five dollars for each copy that is built. Maybe the inventor sells the whole patent to a company that wants to make copies of the invention. If the invention is good, the inventor may make a lot of money from that invention.

But the first step is to get a patent. Without a patent, the inventor has no protection against people who want to make copies of the invention. Getting a patent is very difficult. There are special lawyers who do nothing but get patents for inventors. These lawyers are called patent attorneys. Grandmother Esther explained patents and patent attorneys to Leonard. Then she phoned a patent attorney and told her that Leonard wanted to patent his invention.

Leonard and his grandmother had three meetings with the patent attorney. The attorney answered hundreds of questions. Leonard and Grandmother Esther made diagrams of the invention for her.

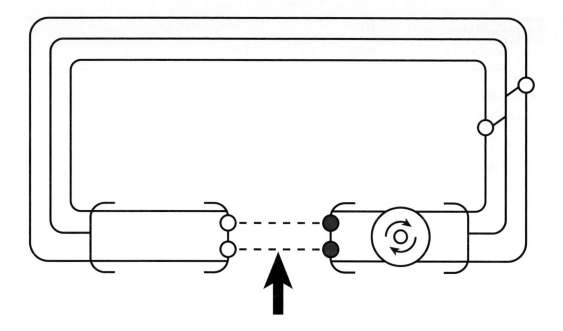

When they finally finished their meetings with the patent attorney, Grandmother Esther said, "Now you owe me another three thousand dollars. If your invention doesn't start making some money, I'll have to give up my flying lessons."

"You're great, Grandma," Leonard said. "You're just great."

"Oh, stop it," Grandmother Esther said and slapped Leonard on the back.

Number your paper from 1 through 25.

C INFORMATION ITEMS

Use the words in the box to write complete sentences.

agreement   sighed   solution   patent   flood

diagram   responded   secret   attorney

1. He ▮▮ to her clever ▮▮ .
2. The ▮▮ ▮▮ wrote an ▮▮ .

3. The solid arrows show how many times people went into the room. How many people went into the room?

4. The dotted arrows show how many times people left the room. How many people left the room?

5. Are the lights on in the room?

6. How many more people would have to leave the room before the lights go off?

Answer these questions about the counter on Leonard's device:

7. Every time somebody goes into the room, what does the counter do?

   - +1   - –1   - –0

8. Every time somebody goes out of the room, what does the counter do?

   - +1   - –1   - –0

9. What number does the counter end up at when the last person leaves the room?

10. What happens to the lights when the counter gets to that number?

For each picture, tell if the lights in the room are **on** or **off**. The solid arrows show people going into the room. The dotted arrows show people leaving the room.

15. Two things happen to melted rock when it moves down the sides of a volcano. Name those 2 things.

16. What is it called when the earth shakes and cracks?

17. The earth makes a circle around the sun one time every ▭ .

18. How many days does it take the earth to make one full circle around the sun?

19. Is it easier to fly alone or with a large flock?

20. Flying near the back of a large flock is like riding your bike ▭ .

   • against the wind   • with the wind

21. During winter at the North Pole, how much does the sun shine?

- all the time
- never

22. During summer at the North Pole, how much does the sun shine?

- all the time
- never

23. When days get shorter, is the North Pole tilting **toward** the sun or **away from** the sun?

24. When days get longer, is the North Pole tilting **toward** the sun or **away from** the sun?

25. In April, the sun shines for more than ___ hours each day in Alaska.

END OF LESSON 46

A

1	2	3
1. <u>basket</u>ball	1. disappointed	1. cloth
2. <u>loud</u>speaker	2. announcer	2. Friday
3. <u>note</u>book	3. smoking	3. prize
4. <u>meant</u>ime	4. manufacturers	4. business
	5. charges	5. cost
	6. hatched	6. forth

B Chapter 11

An Invention Fair

Leonard had found out a lot about inventing things. He found out that you have to start with a need. Then you get an idea for an invention that meets that need. Then you have to build a model of the invention and show that it works. Once you have a model, you must go to a patent attorney and get a patent for your invention. If your invention is the first one of its kind, you'll get a patent. Once you have a patent, you have protection for that invention. Nobody can make copies of the device that you have patented. You can give other people permission to make copies of the invention, but you can charge them for the right to make the copies.

But Leonard was not finished learning about inventions. Once you have patented an invention, you must sell it to somebody who is in the business of making things. Businesses that make things are called manufacturers. Grandmother Esther explained, "There are different ways that we can get in touch with manufacturers. We can take our model and go visit manufacturers who make things for houses. We can call them on the phone and see if they are interested in our invention. We can take out an ad in a magazine that manufacturers read." She shook her head no. Then she smiled and continued. "But there's a better way.

We can put our invention in an invention fair."

"What's an invention fair?" Leonard asked.

His grandmother explained. "An invention fair is a place where inventors and manufacturers get together. The inventors bring their inventions. The manufacturers go to the fair to see if they want any of these new inventions. At the fair there are prizes for the best inventions."

"How soon can we enter an invention fair?" Leonard asked.

Grandmother Esther tossed a magazine to Leonard. It was opened to a large ad. The top of the ad announced, "World's Largest Invention Fair." The rest of the ad told about the prizes and the fair. The first prize was twenty thousand dollars. The second prize was ten thousand dollars. And the third prize was five thousand dollars. There were also special prizes for inventions that were clever.

The fair would start on Friday at noon. Then it would run all day Saturday. It didn't cost inventors anything to show their inventions at the fair. ★ Thousands of people were expected to visit the fair.

Leonard read the ad three times. Each time he read it, the fair sounded greater and greater.

"Can we win?" Leonard asked his grandmother.

"First prize," she said, smiling. "First prize."

Leonard slowly stood up. "You mean we can get twenty thousand dollars for our invention?" Leonard could not even imagine how much money that was. He once saved one hundred dollars. But that wasn't even close to one thousand dollars. As Leonard started to think about twenty <u>thousand</u> dollars, he became a little dizzy. "Twenty thousand dollars," he said over and over.

His grandmother said, "I know you're thinking about twenty thousand dollars, but don't count your chickens before they're hatched."

• • •

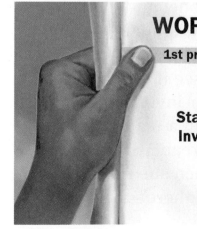

WORLD'S LARGEST INVENTION FAIR

1st prize...$20,000   2nd prize...$10,000   3rd prize $5,000

**Also special prizes for clever inventions
Starts Friday at noon and runs all day Saturday
Inventors—Show your inventions free of charge**

Thousands of people expected to come!

The invention fair took place in a huge hall. Leonard and his grandmother got there early in the morning. The fair opened at noon. Before noon, the inventors had to set up their displays. No inventor could get into the hall before that morning because there had been a basketball game in the hall the evening before. So the inventors were lined up at the door the next morning, ready to set up their displays. Some of them complained about the basketball game. An old man standing near Leonard and his grandmother told them that it would take him six hours to set up his display and he didn't know how he would have it ready when the fair opened. The old man said, "I'll just have to keep working on it while the fair is going on."

The doors opened and the inventors went into the hall. Other large doors opened and trucks moved into the hall. Men jumped from the trucks and began setting up rows and rows of tables. The men covered the tables with cloth. Every now and then a voice came over the loudspeaker and made announcements. One announcement was, "No smoking in the hall." Another announcement told the inventors where their tables were. Each inventor had a blue piece of paper that had a letter and a number on it. The announcer explained to the inventors that all slips that had the letter A would be in the first aisle, that the B's would be in the next aisle, that the C's would be in the next aisle, and so forth. Here's what it said at the top of Leonard's slip: F16.

As Leonard and his grandmother walked to the aisle, Leonard said, "This is the biggest hall I've ever seen in my life."

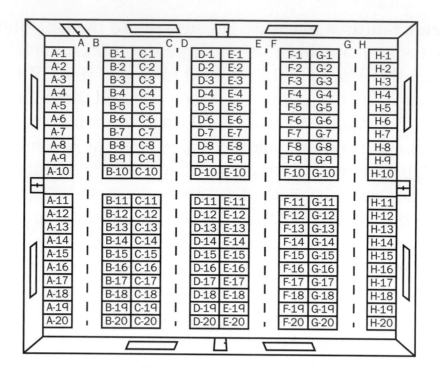

Number your paper from 1 through 26.

STORY ITEMS

Write the words that go in the blanks to tell about the steps Leonard took to invent the electric eye device.

1. He started with a ▢ .

   • solution   • need   • light

   Then he got an idea for an invention.

2. Then he built a ▢ of the invention to show it worked.

3. Then he got a ▢ to protect his invention.

4. What are businesses that make things called?
5. What plan did Grandmother Esther have for getting in touch with these businesses?
   - an invention fair
   - a magazine
   - a lawyer
6. What was first prize at the invention fair?
7. What was second prize?
8. What did Grandmother Esther think they would win?
9. On what day did the fair start?
10. At what time did the fair start?
11. The invention fair was held in a great ____ .
12. Why couldn't the inventors set up their displays the night before the fair?

D REVIEW ITEMS

13. Things closer to the bottom of the pile went into the pile ____ .
14. What does an inventor get to protect an invention?
15. Special lawyers who get protection for inventions are called ____ .
    - doctors
    - patents
    - patent attorneys
16. If other people want to make copies of an invention, they have to make a deal with the ____ .
17. What does the inventor usually make those people do?

18. The solid arrows show how many times people went into the room. How many people went into the room?

19. The dotted arrows show how many times people left the room. How many people left the room?

20. Are the lights on in the room?

21. How many more people would have to leave the room before the lights go off?

22. Write the letter of the earth that has the North Pole tilting away from the sun.

23. Write the letter of the earth that has the North Pole tilting toward the sun.

24. Write the letter of the earth that has darkness all around the North Pole.

25. Write the letter of the earth that has daylight all around the North Pole.

26. Write **A, B, C,** and **D.** Then write the season each earth in the picture shows.

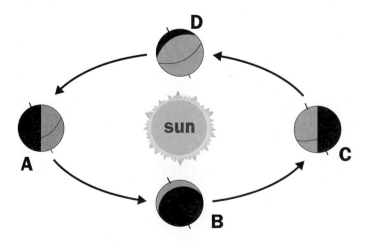

A

1	2	3
1. hesitated	1. interrupted	1. ignore
2. during	2. praised	2. ignoring
3. applause	3. notebooks	3. flood
4. operator	4. disappointed	4. flooding
5. introduced	5. wandering	5. heavy
6. excellent	6. nudged	6. heavily
7. astonishing		

B Chapter 12

The Manufacturers at the Fair

Leonard was very disappointed when the fair opened at noon. He expected to see thousands of people pour into the hall. He imagined that there would be crowds of people looking at his display. But when the fair opened at noon, only a very few people came into the hall.

Only three of the people who came into the hall stopped at Leonard's exhibit. As soon as one of them stopped, Leonard showed how the device worked. For his display he had brought the little room with the doorway. He moved his dolls and stuffed animals into the room. Then he moved them out. He showed how the device worked and explained how the light stays on until everybody has left the room.

But none of the people who stopped at the display that afternoon seemed to be very impressed. Two of them nodded and said, "Very interesting." Then they walked down the F aisle to the next exhibit. The third person who stopped at Leonard's display was a slim woman wearing a gray coat. She didn't say anything. She just looked, listened, nodded her head, and walked away.

Grandmother Esther told Leonard that these people were manufacturers. "They don't seem very interested in the invention," Leonard said.

His grandmother said, "Smart manufacturers never let a cat out of the bag."

Leonard said, "What does that mean?"

She said, "It means they will never let you know what they are really thinking. They will never let you know that they're interested in your invention. They know that you'll want more money for your invention if they're very interested. So they'll act as if they're not very interested. Don't let them fool you. The ones that seem the most interested are the ones who will never want to buy your invention."

"Another thing," his grandmother continued. "A smart manufacturer will try to stay far away from your display. Here's why. The manufacturer doesn't want a crowd to gather in front of your display. The more people who show that they are interested in your invention, the more money the manufacturers will have to pay for your invention. Remember, manufacturers want good inventions, but they don't want to pay any more money than they have to. So they're going to do everything they can to make you think that they're not interested."

After supper, great crowds of people flooded the hall. During most of the evening there was a group of people around Leonard's invention. ★ The people smiled and praised Leonard for his invention.

Grandmother Esther explained, "The people who flood the fair after supper are not manufacturers. These are people who have other jobs. But they want to look at the new inventions. They're coming to the fair after work. The manufacturers have been at this fair since it opened. Being at the fair is part of their job."

"You're really smart, Grandmother," Leonard said.

Grandmother Esther said, "Those people you saw wandering around here this afternoon are the real manufacturers. They're the important ones."

When the fair closed at ten that night, Leonard was very tired. "I never talked so much in my whole life," he explained to his grandmother.

The fair continued on the next day, Saturday. There weren't many people looking at the exhibits early in the morning. Grandmother Esther explained, "Most of the people you see here now are manufacturers. If you watch some of them, you'll see that they're writing things in little notebooks." Leonard watched two people, but neither person wrote anything. Then he spotted the slim woman in the gray coat. She was walking down the G aisle. When the woman got to the end of the aisle, she took out a little book and wrote something. Then she walked to the E aisle and talked to two men. She talked only for a moment. Then the men went one way and she went another way.

"This is really interesting," Leonard said.

Around 11 o'clock that morning, Grandmother Esther said, "Now the manufacturers will have to start making their deals with the inventors."

"Why do they have to make their deals now?" Leonard asked.

Grandmother Esther explained. "First of all, they want to make their deals before the prizes are announced this evening. If the manufacturers think that an invention will win a prize, they know that they can make a much better deal before it gets the prize. Once an invention is a first-prize invention, the inventor can get much more money for the invention."

Leonard said, "But Grandmother, why don't the manufacturers wait until later this afternoon before making deals with the inventors?"

Grandmother Esther said, "Here's the first reason. There will be many people here this afternoon. That means the inventors will be busy explaining their inventions. The second reason is that the manufacturers need at least three hours to make their deals with the inventors."

Number your paper from 1 through 25.

C SKILL ITEMS

The applause interrupted his speech.

1. What word means **broke into?**

2. What word means **the clapping?**

D REVIEW ITEMS

3. Write the letters of the 3 things you find in the Bermuda Triangle.

   a. ice floes   c. whirlpools   e. huge waves

   b. sudden storms   d. streams   f. mountains

4. Which globe shows how the earth looks on the first day of summer?

5. Which globe shows how the earth looks on the first day of winter?

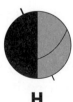
H

sun

J

6. Write the letter of the footprint made by the heaviest animal.

7. Write the letter of the footprint made by the lightest animal.

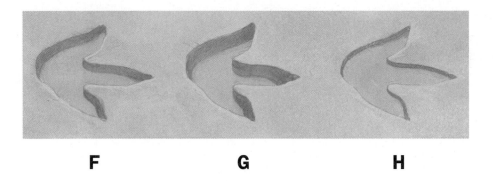

F   **G**   **H**

8. The picture shows marks left by an animal. Which arrow shows the direction the animal is moving?

9. Write the letter of the part that shows a footprint.

10. Write the letter of the part that shows the mark left by the animal's tail.

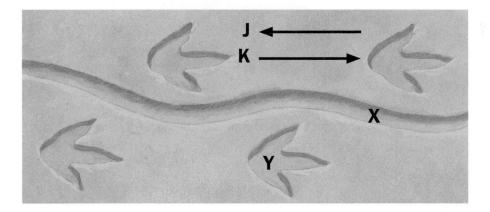

Write the name of each animal in the picture.

11.

12.

13.

14.

15.

16.

17. Which animal in the picture is the smallest?

18. Which animal is the biggest?

19. During which season do ice floes start to melt?

20. During winter in Alaska, you can walk far out on the ocean. Tell why.

21. Do ice floes make noise in the winter?

22. Why do ice floes make noise in the spring?

23. In which direction will you drift when you're in an ocean current?

24. In which direction will you drift when you're in a strong wind?

25. The ▩▩s are the coldest places on the earth and the ▩▩ is the hottest place on the earth.

A

1

1. during
2. elbow
3. hurry
4. involve
5. meantime
6. remind

2

1. products
2. astonishing
3. astonishingly
4. interrupted
5. reasons
6. shorter

3

1. bald
2. boss
3. eleven
4. kindergarten
5. information
6. businesslike

4

1. stage
2. spotlight
3. paused
4. judge
5. deciding
6. introduced

5

1. caked
2. shivered
3. snorted
4. jerked
5. nudged
6. matched

B Chapter 13

Deals

Grandmother Esther had just given two reasons why the manufacturers would try to make deals with inventors before noon. The first reason was that the inventors would be very busy at their displays during the afternoon. The second reason was that it would take time for the inventor and the manufacturer to make a deal.

Just as she finished telling Leonard about what would happen, Leonard noticed that the slim woman in the gray coat was walking toward Leonard's display. She was with a man who was shorter than she was. They stopped at the display next to Leonard's and smiled as they looked at it.

Grandmother Esther whispered, "Leonard, they're going to try to make a deal with us. Let me do all the talking."

✿ The man and woman approached Leonard's display. They stopped. They didn't smile. They just stood there. "Hello," Leonard said at last.

The woman said, "Do you have a patent on this device?"

"Yes," Leonard replied.

The woman said nothing for a few moments. Then she said, "I'm with ABC Home Products." The woman continued, "I don't think many people would be interested in an invention like yours. But I may be able to talk my boss into working out a deal. But that deal must not involve a lot of money."

Grandmother Esther pointed to the large clock in the center of the hall. "It's already after eleven o'clock," she announced loudly. "This afternoon we're ✿ going to be very busy. This evening we're going to win first prize and there will be many manufacturers who are interested in this invention. If you want to make a deal, you'd better start talking about a lot of money and you'd better start right now."

The woman's eyes opened wide. For a moment she didn't seem to know what to say. Then she turned to the man who was with her. He said, "ABC Home Products is a good company to be with. We have a very good name and very good products. That should be important to any inventor."

"We're in no hurry to make a deal," Grandmother Esther said. Then she said, "In fact, I would just as soon wait until after the prizes are announced this evening."

"But what if you don't win first prize?" the man said. "There are some very exciting inventions at this fair. ★ I've looked at ten inventions that could take first prize."

"Well, that's fine," Grandmother Esther said. "You just go and make a deal for one of those inventions. But if you want to talk to us, you can always wait until after we win first prize."

The woman in the gray coat nudged the man with her elbow. The man said, "We're going over to talk to the man we work for. Maybe we'll be back in a few minutes."

The man and woman left. Leonard watched them. They walked very fast toward the C aisle, where another man was standing. In the meantime, three men who had been standing at the head of the F aisle approached Leonard's display. A tall bald man walked up and introduced himself and the two men who were with him. Then he smiled and said, "It's just a shame that our company can't buy your device. I think it's very clever. But we've got too many inventions already. That's a real shame."

One of the other men said to the tall bald man, "Do you think that we might be able to take this invention if we didn't have to pay very much for it?"

The bald man said, "Well, I don't know. I just hadn't thought of that."

The third man said, "I'll bet that we could probably talk our boss into taking it if we didn't have to pay more than a few hundred dollars for it."

The bald man said, "That's an idea I hadn't thought of. Maybe you're right. Maybe we could do that."

Grandmother Esther said, "Who do you think we are, a couple of kindergarten children? You're not going to steal this invention. You're going to tell us the name of the company you're with. You're going to give us your business card. You're going to tell us your best deal. And then we're going to see if that deal is better than the deal ABC Home Products wants to make."

"But Grandma," Leonard said. He was going to remind her that ABC Home Products had not told about the deal they wanted to make.

She interrupted Leonard and said, "I know what you're thinking, Leonard. You want to go with ABC Home Products. But we have to give these other manufacturers a chance, too."

Number your paper from 1 through 25.

C SKILL ITEMS

Use the words in the box to write complete sentences you have learned.

company	applause	owed	patent	connected
attorney	prize	agreement	interrupted	

1. The ▮▮ ▮▮ wrote an ▮▮ .
2. The ▮▮ ▮▮ his speech.

D REVIEW ITEMS

3. What are clouds made of?

4. What kind of cloud does the picture show?

5. What happens to a drop of water at **B**?

6. What is a person doing when the person makes an object for the first time?

7. The person who makes an object for the first time is called an ▮▮ .

8. The object the person makes is called an ▮▮ .

9. What are businesses that make things called?

10. Geese live in large groups called ▨ .

11. Where are most wild geese born?

12. In which direction do geese fly in the fall?

13. What is this trip called?

Choose from these words to answer each item:

- moon
- equator
- Florida
- geese
- sun
- poles
- Canada
- migration

14. The heat that the earth receives comes from the ▨ .

15. The part of the earth that receives more heat than any other part is the ▨ .

16. The parts of the earth that receive less heat than any other part are called the ▨ .

17. Which letter shows the part of the earth that receives **more** heat from the sun than any other part?

18. Which letter shows a part of the earth that receives **less** heat from the sun than any other part?

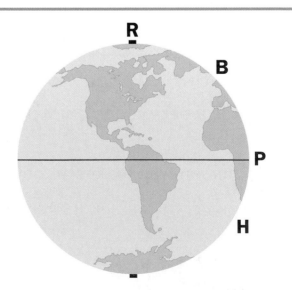

19. If you cannot see the sun, is it **daytime** or **nighttime** on your side of the earth?

20. What is it on the other side of the earth?

21. The earth turns around one time every [   ] hours.

22. Write the letter of the earth that shows the person in daytime.

23. Write the letter of the earth that shows the person 6 hours later.

24. Write the letter that shows the person another 6 hours later.

25. Write the letter that shows the person another 6 hours later.

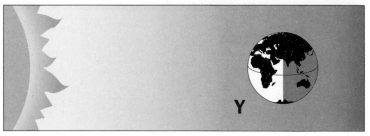

END OF LESSON 49

A

1

1. ragged
2. boar
3. bristles
4. bristling
5. nostrils

2

1. rigid
2. linger
3. glide
4. briars
5. astonishingly

3

1. tremble
2. trembling
3. flung
4. splinter
5. splintery
6. blood
7. damp

4

1. spilling
2. thorns
3. confusing
4. scarred
5. absolutely
6. bluejays

5

1. teaberry
2. twirl
3. terror
4. glistened
5. stiff

Boar Out There

Written by Cynthia Rylant, Illustrated by Rick Drennan

Everyone in Glen Morgan knew there was a
wild boar in the woods over by the Miller farm.
The boar was out beyond the splintery rail
fence and past the old black Dodge that
somehow had ended up in the woods and was
missing most of its parts.

Jenny would hook her chin over the top rail of the fence, twirl a long green blade of grass in her teeth and whisper, "Boar out there."

And there were times she was sure she heard him. She imagined him running heavily through the trees, ignoring the sharp thorns and briars that raked his back and sprang away trembling.

She thought he might have a golden horn on his terrible head. The boar would run deep into the woods, then rise up on his rear hooves, throw his head toward the stars and cry a long, clear, sure note into the air. The note would glide through the night and spear the heart of the moon. The boar had no fear of the moon, Jenny knew, as she lay in bed, listening.

One hot summer day she went to find the boar. No one in Glen Morgan had ever gone past the old black Dodge and beyond, as far as she knew. But the boar was there somewhere, between those awful trees, and his dark green eyes waited for someone.

Jenny felt it was she.

Moving slowly over damp brown leaves, Jenny could sense her ears tingle and fan out as she listened for thick breathing from the trees. She stopped to pick a teaberry leaf to chew, stood a minute, then went on.

Deep in the woods she kept her eyes to the sky. She needed to be reminded that there was a world above and apart from the trees—a world of space and air, air that didn't linger all about her, didn't press deep into her skin, as forest air did.

Finally, leaning against a tree to rest, she heard him for the first time. She forgot to breathe, standing there listening to the stamping of hooves, and she choked and coughed.

Coughed!

And now the pounding was horrible, too
loud and confusing for Jenny. Horrible. She
stood stiff with wet eyes and knew she could
always pray, but for some reason didn't.

He came through the trees so fast that she
had no time to scream or run. And he was
there before her.

His large gray-black body shivered as he waited
just beyond the shadow of the tree she held for
support. His nostrils glistened, and his eyes; but
astonishingly, he was silent. He shivered and
glistened and was absolutely silent.

Jenny matched his silence, and her body was
rigid, but not her eyes. They traveled along his
scarred, bristling back to his thick hind legs. Tears
spilling and flooding her face, Jenny stared at the
boar's ragged ears, caked with blood. Her tears
dropped to the leaves, and the only sound
between them was his slow breathing.

Then the boar snorted and jerked. But Jenny did not move.

High in the trees a bluejay yelled, and, suddenly, it was over. Jenny stood like a rock as the boar wildly flung his head and in terror bolted past her.

Past her . . .

And now, since that summer, Jenny still hooks her chin over the old rail fence, and she still whispers, "Boar out there." But when she leans on the fence, looking into the trees, her eyes are full and she leaves wet patches on the splintery wood. She is sorry for the torn ears of the boar and sorry that he has no golden horn.

But mostly she is sorry that he lives in fear of bluejays and little girls, when everyone in Glen Morgan lives in fear of him.

Little House on the Prairie

Laura Ingalls Wilder

Vocabulary Sentences

Lessons 1–50

1. The horses became restless on the dangerous route.

2. Scientists do not ignore ordinary things.

3. She actually repeated that careless mistake.

4. The smell attracted flies immediately.

5. The rim of the volcano exploded.

6. The new exhibit displayed mysterious fish.

7. She automatically arranged the flowers.

8. They were impressed by her large vocabulary.

9. He responded to her clever solution.

10. The patent attorney wrote an agreement.

11. The applause interrupted his speech.

12. She selected a comfortable seat.

Fact Game Answer Keys

2. a. T
b. north

3. a. R
b. T

4. a. M
b. B

5. a. Q
b. R

6. a. F
b. M
c. Q

7. A — summer
B — fall
C — winter
D — spring

8. a. year
b. 365 days
c. 5

9. a. three years old
b. until one goose dies; for life
c. about 30 years

10. a. south
b. north

11. a. Y
b. Y
c. A

12. a. J
b. P

Fact Game for Test 2

2. a. spring
b. spring

3. a. north
b. west
c. south

4. a. J
b. F

5. a. away from the sun
b. toward the sun

6. a. winter
b. summer

7. a. B
b. G

8. a. T
b. P

9. a. X
b. P and T

10. a. Ideas: (any three) fish, ants, snakes, frogs, and so on
b. Ideas: (any three) bears, humans, dogs, cows, horses, cats, whales, and so on

11. a. no
    b. warm-blooded

12. a. not warm; cold
    b. 12

Fact Game for Test 3

2. a. C
   b. B

3. a. water; currents
   b. funnel

4. a. dinosaurs
   b. horses

5. a. C
   b. D

6. a. A
   b. B
   c. D

7. a. D
   b. Mesozoic

8. a. D
   b. D
   c. C

9. A. Triceratops
   B. Tyrannosaurus

10. a. dinosaurs
    b. earlier; first

11. a. (tiny) drops of water
    b. storm cloud

12. A, D, E

Fact Game for Test 4

2. a. shoe
   b. rock

3. a. rock
   b. cup

4. R

5. 1800

6. pens, paper, shoes, houses, stoves

7. a. inventor
   b. invention

8. a. need
   b. figure out how to meet that need

9. to get places faster; to use shorter routes

10. millions of years ago

11. earthquake

12. It cools and gets hard.

Fact Game for Test 5

2. a. 2
b. 2

3. a. into the room
b. out of the room

4. A — on
B — off
C — off
D — on

5. a. need
b. model
c. patent

6. manufacturers

7. a. yes
b. 2

8. a. patent
b. patent attorneys

9. a. counts forward; +1
b. counts backward; -1

10. a. outside beam
b. inside beam
c. on

11. a. off
b. on

12. a. zero
b. They turn off.